Daily Manna From The Psalms

Nuggets of Hope for the Hungry Christian

Leah D. Jackson

Dedication

*To all the disciples on life's journey who are seeking to transform the
world while being transformed by the power of God.*

Sandra,

May the journey of this
book lead you to places that
you never imagined. I pray
that God speaks to your heart
as you read.

Love,

Bea 12/13

Introduction

Life can be a trip. Literally a journey taking you from coast-to-coast, ocean-to-ocean, state-to-state, and country-to-country. It lifts you up to highest mountains and then drags you down all the way to and through the lowest valleys. It allows you to fly high, up above the clouds, and then causes you to sink down to the bottom of the ocean floor. It leads you through yellow and orange days, full of excitement and celebration. It takes you through green and purple days, full of hope and promise. It drops you off on blue and grey days in the depths of sorrow and despair. And finally drives you to red and pink days filled with passion and love. Life can be a trip!

I have learned that no matter where life takes me, the Book of Psalms always has something for me. Each time that I place my key in their door, something almost magical greets me at the entryway to encourage me, guide me, strengthen me, rebuke me, challenge me, convict me, or comfort me. God continuously speaks and reveals Himself through the passages of this encyclopedia of scriptures, written by different authors, at different times, in different places, and under very different circumstances. One would think that these differences would result in a disjointed mess, and maybe that would be the case if this was a regular 'ol collection of writings, prepared by uninspired people, with no purpose, or anointing. However, the Book of Psalms, like all scripture are sacred, holy, and God inspired. Each psalm joins with the others to fulfill the purpose for which God sent them.

"All Scripture is God-breathed and is useful for teaching, rebuking, correcting and training in righteousness, so that the servant of God may be thoroughly equipped for every good work" (2 Timothy 2:16-17). Each time I pick up the Psalms I am equipped. Not simply by the words on the page, but the revelation that the Holy Spirit deposits into my heart and mind. That is the beauty of reading the Word devotionally and not simply educationally; God provides unique revelation just for us. Yes we want to know the Word of God, but why? Is it that we are pursuing academic knowledge? Not really. Is it that we want to know God theoretically? That isn't quite right either. We are in pursuit of intimacy with God, knowledge of God, and understanding of our lives; God's will and plan for us, and the circumstances surrounding us. We desire revelation.

This book is intended to provide you with a daily nugget from the heart of God to guide you in your daily pursuit of God and the things of God. I pray that as you read this devotional that God will meet you each day and that you will walk away with a piece of revelation that will help you grow as you go. Take the time to read this book devotionally. Take the time to read the daily psalm slowly, allowing the words to sink in and time for God to speak to your mind, heart, and spirit. Then read the daily devotional entry, taking the time to complete any exercise provided that day. After you complete your daily entry, pray this simple prayer:

God,
As I step away from this time with you, allow the words of this psalm and this devotional to minister to me throughout the remainder of this day. Give me the courage to apply your Word to my life and to allow this revelation to draw me closer to you, to propel me into my destiny, and to become the man or woman that you desire for me to become. I love you Lord!

In Jesus Name,
Amen

Psalm 1

Psalm 1, a Hebrew Poem, paints a picture of two very different individuals. On one side of the canvas is "Righteous" and on the other is "Wicked." Righteous and Wicked have very different characteristics. The psalmist gives us instructions for Godly living and warns us of the repercussions of choosing the wrong path while contrasting the attributes of these people.

Verse 2 tells us that Righteous delights in the law of the Lord. To delight means to take pleasure in and to rejoice with. Not only does the law of the Lord bring the Righteous person pleasure, this individual's purpose is found in God's law as well. When something delights us, we become preoccupied with it and we tend to protect and guard it. It is valuable to us. God's Word is central to the Righteous person's life. This person meditates on the Word continuously, day and night. Righteous does not take a haphazard approach to the Word, but instead studying it is a key purpose and affair in their life, an activity to which they pay careful attention. Reading, reflecting on, and studying God's Word is not something that Righteous squeezes in after teeth brushing or even during half time while watching the game. No, Righteous talks about God's law when she sits at home and when she walks along the road, when she lies down and when she gets up, just as God instructs her to do in Deuteronomy 6:7. As a result of the Righteous person's steadfast devotion to God and his Word, this person finds a stable foundation for their life.

The description of the Wicked person begins in verse 4. The psalm writer simply says that everything that the Righteous person is, Wicked is not. Where Righteous delights in the law of the Lord, Wicked does not. When Righteous meditates on God's law day and night, while the Wicked person does not. Righteous is stable, rooted, and planted, not Wicked. When one is stable, rooted, and planted they are like a tree. The roots of a tree runs deep so that it can withstand rain, hail, and wind. The Righteous may experience trials, but they are anchored in God and will not waver. Righteous is fruitful and enjoys the fruit of his connection to God, but Wicked has no fruit.

Now think about your close friends. Are they more like Righteous or the Wicked? The Word repeatedly warns us about the significance of the company we keep. Proverbs 22:24-25 instructions us, "do not make friends with a hot-tempered man, do not associate with one easily angered, or *you may learn his ways and get yourself ensnared*" (emphasis mine). Birds of a feather flock together. Who are you walking, standing, or sitting with? These are your true teachers.

The people we choose to befriend or allow to befriend us have an impact on our present and our future. Whether we choose to walk with Righteous or Wicked can change the course of our lives forever. As James 3:5-6 reminds us, an entire forest is set ablaze by the impact of one spark. Our lives, our paths, and our destinies are like that forest; the course of them can be forever changed by the influence of Righteous or Wicked. Who is shaping your future?

Psalm 2

This Royal Psalm continues the proclamation of blessedness that began in Psalm 1. The previous psalm promises that those who delight in the law of the Lord and avoid walking in the counsel of the wicked will be blessed. Psalm 2 proclaims that those who acknowledge God's lordship (and that of His anointed) and take refuge in Him will be blessed. Ahh, the promises of God; they are so sweet.

In order to reap the rewards found in the conditional promises of God, we must first go through the precepts of God. If we acknowledge God's lordship THEN we will be blessed. The writer of Psalm 2 teaches us that God's precepts and His promises go hand in hand.

The writer of this psalm reflects on an established Biblical precept, *the people of God must submit to human authority because God establishes all authority* (e.g. Romans 13:1). At the time that this psalm was written, a new king was coming into power and a segment of the population rebelled against him. They conspired and plotted against the king and met secretly to voice their opposition (vs. 1-3). Tsk, tsk, tsk. How could they act this way, you ask. Wait--before you judge your brothers and sisters of old too harshly, take a quick look in the mirror.

Do you respect those in authority over you? Your parents? Your boss? Your pastor? Your team captain? Your club president? Do you submit to the leadership of others, even when they weren't YOUR choice? What about those you don't like, do you follow them or do you gossip about them, thwart their leadership, or try to take over?

To rebel against those that the Lord has anointed equals rebellion against God. The writer of Psalm 2 reveals to us that when we oppose, disobey, defy or otherwise rebel against those in leadership, it angers the Lord (vs. 5). Why? Because by doing so, we have rejected God and questioned His perfect will to rule, lead, and govern us. God is the ultimate judge, king, and head of all things. Just as God created the earth, the animals and humanity, the Lord is also in control of all things (Isaiah 45:7).

This includes the plan for your life, which God ordained before the foundation of the world. Accepting the lordship of God also means accepting His plans and those He anoints and appoints. Even when it doesn't make sense, you must "trust in the Lord with all your heart, and do not lean on your own understanding," that includes respecting and submitting to those in leadership (Proverbs 3:5).

Take refuge in God. Trust that He is concerned about everything that concerns you, including those who have authority over you. Just as God has numbered the hairs on your head, He knows the thoughts, motives, and actions of those in authority. He will not allow them to harm you. Place your hope and trust in God and not man today. You're covered!

Psalm 3

This psalm has come to be associated with David as he was running from his son Absalom who was trying to overthrow him as king. Although it is unlikely that David actually wrote this lament, this cry to God from the psalmist expresses the spirit of the situation that David experienced in 2 Samuel 15-18. I can only imagine the sea of emotions that David felt as he had to mentally re-categorize his son, his own flesh and blood, from friend to foe. Having enemies is often arduous and disappointing, but discovering that your son is among them had to be devastating for David.

Although threatened and devastated by the attacks of his foes, the psalmist cried aloud to the Lord. The writer told God exactly what was going on in his life. Many are my foes; they rise up against me; people are mocking (vs. 1-2). Who do you turn to when your enemies attack? When people attempt to tarnish your name? We often run to our friends, family members, or other loved ones when things go wrong, but they lack the power, influence, or resources to help us. And when they are incapable of solving our problems, we find ourselves even more disappointed, hurt, and lost than we were before we turned to them. Proverbs 3:5-6 instructs us to "Trust in the Lord with all your heart and lean not on your own understanding; in all your ways submit to him, and he will make your paths straight." We cannot trust in God and His plans and then turn to humans as the source of our answers, comfort, and provision at the same time.

The psalmist trusted in and turned to God, knowing that only Yahweh was His protector and sustainer. Verses 3 and 4 say, "but YOU are a shield around me, O Lord; YOU bestow glory on me and lift up my head. To the Lord I cry aloud, and HE answers me from HIS holy hill" (emphasis mine). The writer was not only confident that the Lord had his back, but also that the Lord would respond to his cry and therefore he had nothing to fear (vs. 5-6). In our darkest hours we have nothing to fear if we are truly confident in God's ability to protect and deliver us.

This psalm continues with a bold approach to the throne of grace, calling forth immediate action from God. ARISE LORD! DELIVER ME! The writer is so confident in his relationship with God that he commands God to respond. We too have the ability to go boldly to God with our petitions. God promises in Matthew 7:7-9 to respond to specific requests if we but ask, knock and seek... What need is going unmet in your life because you aren't bold enough to ASK?! Take your need to God today and leave it with Him, knowing that He is "able to do immeasurably more than all we ask or imagine, according to his power that is at work within us" (Ephesians 3:20).

Psalm 4

Today, the psalmist seeks the Lord when falsely accused by slanders. This prayer opens with a cry for help and a clear explanation of what is needed in this situation; relief from distress, mercy and a response. When you seek the face of God through prayer, are you clear about exactly what you want from God? When you cry out, HELP ME LORD, do you know what kind of "help" you are looking for? Do you need God to pay your light bill? Then say, pay this light bill, Lord. Do you need healing in your liver? Then say, heal my liver Lord. Do you need a promotion to district manager of packaging on your job? Then say just that. Be confident enough in God's ability and willingness to respond to you and your needs to pray with specificity. Psalm 102:17 promises that "He will respond to the prayer of the destitute; he will not despise their plea"--but what EXACTLY is your plea?

When the prophet Elijah was facing Ahab and the prophets of Baal on Mount Carmel in 1 Kings 18 he acted boldly, specifically, and with confidence that God would respond. Elijah challenged the prophets of Baal to have their god bring forth fire on their altar. When their god failed to respond, Elijah mocked them and then confidently set up his own altar before Yahweh. Elijah was so confident that HIS GOD could and would respond that he had his altar drenched with water three times and then he presented his plea to God. Like the psalmist, Elijah knew exactly what he needed and expected from God, FIRE! And Elijah asked for fire. He did not ask for God's will in the situation. He did not ask for God to move in some unspecified way. He did not ask for money, healing, food, or other things, he asked for fire when he needed fire.

After the psalmist presented his request confidently and precisely in Psalm 4, he laid down in peace (vs. 7-8). There was nothing left for him to be anxious about, because his situation was now in the master's hands. No matter the circumstances you face in this season, you too can find rest for your mind, heart, and soul when you are confident in God and His ability. Our God is the God of shalom (peace). My brothers and sisters, "Be anxious for nothing, but in everything by prayer and supplication with thanksgiving let your requests be made known to God. And the peace of God, which surpasses all comprehension, shall guard your hearts and your minds in Christ Jesus" (Philippians 4:6-7).

Psalm 5

I came across this scripture on the "right day." I am in a season where it seems like I add an individual to my list of foes almost daily, so this passage is right on time. Have you ever found yourself in a place where you didn't know who you could trust? Have you wondered who is on your side? Have you ever questioned if you have a friend in anyone, other than Jesus? If so, you are not alone. I understand your feelings of discomfort, loneliness, vulnerability, and uncertainty during these times.

Like David, I wake up and cry out to the Lord for help (vs. 2), because I don't know what to do. Since my enemies seem so numerous, I don't know where the landmines are around me. God should I step here or there? Should I go right or left? Uncertainty has become normative, so I ask the Lord to lead and guide me down the path that He has ordained for me (vs. 8). This uncertainty has reminded me of my total dependence on God. Self-reliance can be tempting, but there is a more perfect way; there is a promise of God for me to stand on and this promise is for you too. Proverbs 3:5-6 instructs us to "trust in the Lord with all your heart and lean not on your own understanding; in all your ways acknowledge him and he will direct your path."

In the midst of times where our foes attack, we can find strength in vs. 12, "surely, Lord, you bless the righteous; you surround them with your favor as with a shield." Ahh, here is a promise with a hidden command. If we are found righteous then God will surround us with His shield of favor. Instead of worrying about our enemies, we need to focus on being righteous; it is through righteousness that we will find the protection of God's favor.

If you find yourself identifying with the psalmist (and me) today, pray this prayer:

Lord help me to be righteous in your eyes. Right standing before you God, is what I desire and need most of all. It is because of my righteousness that I will be blessed with the covering of your favor and be shielded from the attacks of my enemies. In Jesus name, Amen.

Psalm 6

In 1982, Annie sang that the "sun will come out tomorrow," but what happens when it doesn't? Sometimes we can want a situation to change overnight, but that doesn't mean that it will. We cry out to God until our pillows are covered with tears and still wake up the next morning and realize that neither the season nor circumstance has changed. Ugh! Been there? I think we all have. This is where David found himself in Psalm 6; He was simply over it!

David was worn out from his groaning (vs. 6). He was sick and tired of being sick and tired. Tired of praying about the same thing. Sick of his present reality. Disgusted by the fact that he was still going through the same 'ol thing, so he cried out to the Lord for mercy. Requesting mercy from God is a cry for God to demonstrate His compassion towards you. Not because you deserve it, but because of God's nature. God is loving, sympathetic, compassionate, charitable, and kind. God is also merciful. To ask God for mercy, particularly in the face of hardship, is the recognition of God's power and sovereignty. Isaiah 45:5-7 teaches us that God is in control of everything, including everything in the present and the future. A cry for mercy is a request for God to bring about change, to give you what you do not deserve in a situation that He ultimately has control over. Who besides the Lord has that type of power? Who else can bring about change in your life? In your situation? In your future?

I am encouraged by David's infinite trust in God during this time of darkness. He knows that God will answer him and grant his request of mercy, even before it is evident, even before his prayer has ended. "The Lord has heard my cry for mercy; the Lord accepts my prayer" (vs. 9). That is serious trust in God and in his relationship with God. Do you trust God THAT much? Maybe, just maybe, if we can learn to trust God more, we will see a change in our situations. Instead of praying about your situation today, ask God to increase your trust in Him.

Psalm 7

Here we find the psalmist still under attack from his enemies. I know it may seem a bit overwhelming to you that this individual is still crying out to the Lord about his foes.

We must keep in mind that all the psalms were not written by the same individual, so we're possibly looking at cries of protection from various people. But what if we weren't? What if all of these "save me" letters to God were pinned by the same psalmist? Then this collection of writings would be a good reflection of our everyday lives.

How many times have you found yourself dealing with similar situations? So much so that it feels like déjà vu? Our God is not random; we do not just go through things without reason. Much of what we experience is to prepare us for what is to come. "Consider it pure joy, my brothers and sisters, whenever you face trials of many kinds, because you know that the testing of your faith produces perseverance. Let perseverance finish its work so that you may be mature and complete, not lacking anything" (James 1:2-4). The adversity that we face teaches us to endure, to persevere, and to stand. Jesus told us in John 16:33 that we would face trials and that we would overcome them. Overcoming one time, teaches you how to overcome the next, and then again the time after that. The difficulties that we endure and overcome today help us to build our spiritual muscles for tomorrow. No pain, no gain! Right?

I faced a difficult enemy many years ago. I was under constant attack by this individual. Lies were spread. Threats were made. All the strategies of intimidation were used. He even rallied others against me. This was a very difficult and LONG season to endure. A great deal of prayer and fasting went into trying to overcome. Many tears were shed and a lot of journals were used, but I overcame. I never thought that I would have reason to thank God for such a difficult time, but I have. That experience, not only drew me closer to God and taught me a great deal about practicing the spiritual disciplines, but it made facing other enemies that much easier. Why? Because I knew God had delivered me from my enemy before and therefore He would do it again. "And we know that in all things God works for the good of those who love him, who have been called according to his purpose" (Romans 8:28). What has God worked together for your good? What situations did He bring you through? He's done it before and therefore He will do it again. For this reason, we can join the psalmist and pray with confidence "O righteous God, who searches minds and hearts, bring to an end the violence of the wicked and make the righteous secure" (vs. 9).

As you go through, say to yourself, "don't fret, God is simply creating material to be used for my good." Stand firm in the confidence that "you win." Every time, you win!

Psalm 8

Coming behind several desperate cries to the Lord for deliverance from enemies, this psalm is a bit refreshing. The psalmist stands in awe of the majesty of the Lord, which brings him to a place of complete humility. The writer seems to be singing to a different tune; a brighter one. Is it because all of the troubles of yesterday no longer exist in his world? Or because his enemies have finally been silenced? No. The superscription (introductory words) for the text tells us that this psalm is to be sang according to *gittith*, which in Hebrew refers to a winepress. This is a song of the winepress. Trust me, there is nothing bright or chipper about the winepress, especially if you are the grape!

The winepress was made of two receptacles, one where the grapes were crushed and another where the juice was captured. The only way to get wine is for the grape to be bruised, pressed, and crushed. Often times, the children of God are placed in the same position as grapes. We must endure pressure for the good stuff inside of us to be released. This psalmist was praising God in the winepress, in the midst of his testing. His message is very clear; the Lord is worthy of praise!

The psalmist tells of the majesty of the Lord. The Hebrew word for majesty captures splendor, beauty, excellence, glory, sovereignty, and honor that are characteristic of God. His majesty extends to and embraces the entire earth and all its inhabitants; it reaches to the heavens and all its inhabitants. The magnitude of God's sovereignty creates a sense of wonder and awe within the hearts and minds of humans, because it is truly beyond our ability to comprehend.

When I think of the majesty of God, I am reminded of Jesus' imperative in Matthew 18:3, "truly I tell you, unless you change and become like little children, you will never enter the kingdom of heaven." Young children are amazed, excited, and wowed every day not by the big things, but the small things. As they eat their favorite foods they exclaim, "Mommy, this is the best dinner EVER." As they run on the playground they laugh and squeal, putting everything they have into their work—play. A rainy day turns into a day of adventure as they explore new

14

games and activities within their own homes. Each and every day for a little child is an exploration of the majesty of God.

Pray with me: *God, give us the eyes of a little child so that we can see and then appreciate the majesty of all you are and have created. Amen.*

Psalm 9

This Psalm of Thanksgiving begins with a commitment by the psalmist to praise God with all of his heart. This statement was not simply a promise of positive emotion or affection directed towards God, but rather a statement regarding the psalmist's entire being. Biblical references to the heart have a much wider scope than just to the organ; it is the center of the physical, mental, and spiritual life of humans. We think, act, and feel from our hearts (See Matthew 6:21, Proverbs 3:5, 2 Corinthians 9:7, Proverbs 4:23). In verse 1 of today's psalm, the writer commits to praise God with everything within him.

The writer could have stopped with his commitment to praise God with his entire life; however, it seems he wanted to clarify that he would not keep his praise to himself, but that he would tell others of the wonders of the Lord. In the Book of Psalms, praise and thanksgiving are rarely a private matter, but instead are public acts. The psalms are so intimate that it often seems that we are reading the writers' journal entries, but we are usually reading public professions made in the assembly. In Psalm 9, the writer says that God is so wonderful, incredible, and awesome that I cannot keep it to myself. He must tell someone else. Anybody. EVERYBODY! Is this how you feel about God?

Who are you telling? Who are you sharing your story with? Who knows how good God has been to you? What attributes of God's character has He revealed to you? What blessings has God bestowed upon you? Here, the writer of this psalm is summoning us, calling us, beckoning us to join him in praising God. We are being called to joyfully declare the wonder and works of the Lord in our lives, just as the psalm writers have done. The stories of the faith lead us, guide us, encourage us, and help us to know God better. What insight about God or piece of encouragement are the people in your sphere of influence missing out on because you haven't told your story? Because you have not publicly declared the praise of God? Because you haven't joined the writer of Psalm 9 in singing the praise of the Most High? Your praise is necessary. Make a commitment to share your story TODAY!

Psalm 10

Today, the psalm writer spends a significant amount of time illuminating the dreadful actions of the wicked man. Among other things, he preys on the weak, is boastful, prideful, and arrogant, encourages greed, and victimizes and murders others. Although this psalm was written thousands of years ago, its characterization of the wicked still rings true today. We do not have to look far to see that we are surrounded by wickedness. As I write this reflection, the headlines in the newspaper include stories of: a 6 month-old baby that was shot and killed in Chicago while having her diaper changed, a 13 year-old boy in Atlanta who is holding his family hostage after stealing 2 vehicles this morning, a 26 year-old teacher in New Orleans has been missing for 2 weeks after celebrating a Teacher of the Year nomination, and the former mayor of the city of Detroit is returning to jail on corruption charges. Our nation and our world are full of wickedness.

Unfortunately, sin begets sin. One sin leads to the next sin, which leads to a pattern or life of sin. When this occurs, we find ourselves in a vicious cycle of sin. First John 3:4 teaches us that sin is lawlessness (i.e. breaking God's law) and Deuteronomy 9:7 defines sin as disobedience or rebellion against God. Ultimately, sin separates us from God (see Isaiah 59:2). Continuation of an unchecked sinful existence results in wickedness; lack of concern for the Lord and total disregard of God. According to the writer of Psalm 10, the wicked operate out of arrogance instead of humility (vs. 2). He is also disillusioned. Look at verse 11, "he says to himself, "God has forgotten; he covers his face and never sees." And now, verse 13 "he won't call me to account." This arrogant presumption of the wicked is not only self-indulgent, but also contrary to biblical witness. Job 28:24 says, "For he looks to the ends of the earth and sees everything under the heavens." There is nothing occurring on this earth that God does not see or look to see. This passage from Job indicates that God actively looks upon the earth to take inventory of what is occurring. God is not only watching us, but will hold us accountable on the Day of Judgment for our actions (See Matthew 12:36 and Hebrews 4:13).

If you find yourself on the receiving end of wickedness or a wicked person's schemes, do not fret. This text is full of many promises of God made just for you:

- Verse 14- God sees your trouble; God grieves over your trouble; God takes on your cause personally; God is your helper
- Verse 16- God is ruler and reigns forever; the wicked will perish
- Verse 17- God will encourage you, God hears your cry, God will defend you, you do not have to be afraid, the wicked are not God and ultimately are no threat to you

Remember this today: The Lord is King forever and ever...not the wicked! The wicked may seem to succeed today, but they will have their day in court. They will go before the King of kings and the Lord of the lords.

Psalm 11

In this Psalm of David we seem to be overhearing a conversation between the writer and a friend. I can envision how this scene played out. David turned to a friend in the midst of crisis (probably running from Saul or Absalom) expressing belief that the Lord would deliver him from his enemies and his friend replied in an unexpected fashion. Instead of providing the writer with encouragement to hang in there, stand firm, and trust completely in God, his friend told him to "flee like a bird" (vs. 1). What?!

How often has this happened to you? You turned to a friend for comfort, encouragement, or sound advice and received foolishness instead. It's happened to me many times. I run to someone for help and end up encouraging myself. It is often easy to turn to other human beings for counsel and support because we can see them, we can hear them, and we can touch them. But humans are flesh and blood, just like us. They can only speak revelation, if God gives it to them. Hence the reason the writer of Psalm 118:8 says, "it is better to take refuge in the Lord than to trust in humans." Like many of us, the psalm writer learned this lesson the hard way. After his friend could not meet his needs, the writer of Psalm 11 ended up testifying to his apprehensive friend in the midst of his need for assistance.

Make a commitment today to go to God first. God will supply all of your needs (Philippians 4:19). God will either speak the answer you need directly to you or direct you to the person that He has assigned to help you with your circumstance. Don't waste your time, particularly during a time of vulnerability, talking to anyone before you seek the Lord.

The writer begins with a declaration that the Lord is his refuge and ends with a declaration that God is righteous. As a result of these truths, David knows that he has nothing to fear. His enemies can bend their bows, set their arrows, or even take their best shot at him (vs. 2), but God is still in control and will protect him. Do you have that type of unshakable faith in God? Do you believe that God will protect you against injustice? If not, ask God to help your unbelief.

Psalm 12

Today, we have a Prayer of David; he cries out, "Help, Lord, for the godly are no more." Yes, he is petitioning God again about the behavior of evildoers. But before you get irritated with David for what seems like a preoccupation with the same issue, STOP! Can you really blame him? Have you ever had an issue that seemed to drag on and on? I'm in the midst of one now. At this moment, I am experiencing day 4 of a stomach virus. Four days of all the grossness associated with a stomach bug. Four days without an appetite. Four days of sports drinks, ginger ale, and saltine crackers. Four days in the bed. Do you think that I have stopped praying for healing, just because this has gone on for 96 hours? My issue, though presently all consuming, is not nearly as serious as the circumstances of David's life. He fought a giant that was insulting the Lord and bullying God's people (1 Samuel 17), and he ran away from Saul (1 Samuel 21) and from his son Absalom (2 Samuel 15-18) to save his life. David had some serious enemies to contend with, so I am willing to give him as many prayers and journal entries as he needs to cry out to God.

I must admit, as I read verses 3 and 4 that I chuckled a bit. David was complaining to the Lord that his enemies "talk too much." It is as if he was saying, it is one thing to have enemies and to have to run from them, but all of that boasting, bragging, and taunting is just too much! I can hear him saying, "Shut them up, Lord!" I am sure that their endless chatter made David angry, just as the words of Goliath did in 1 Samuel 17:8-10, "Why do you come out and line up for battle? Am I not a Philistine, and are you not the servants of Saul? Choose a man and have him come down to me. If he is able to fight and kill me, we will become your subjects; but if I overcome him and kill him, you will become our subjects and serve us. ...This day I defy the armies of Israel! Give me a man and let us fight each other." This taunting caused David to become righteously indignant and go after Goliath.

Whoa, doggie! Before you strap up to go after all your enemies, take a pause for the cause and run to the Lord, as David did in Psalm 12. Seek the Lord before you act. The enemy may be trying to provoke you to act hastily; do not give him any glory. When your enemy throws insults your way, remember this: "Do

21

not be quickly provoked in your spirit, for anger resides in the lap of fools" (Ecclesiastes 7:9).

"Fools give full vent to their rage, but the wise bring calm in the end." (Proverbs 29:11) The best way to regain your composure and to remain righteous is to RUN to God in prayer. When we take our needs and particularly the attacks of our enemies to God, God always responds; Psalm 12 was no exception. God answered David's prayer in verses 5 and 6, with a promise to ARISE and PROTECT him from his enemies and their slanderous words. You see, the battle was never David's to begin with and it is not yours either. Get out of your own way and God's way and allow Jehovah Nissi (the Lord your banner) to fight your battles.

Psalm 13

This Psalm of David is characterized as a lament, and with good reason. It follows the classic pattern of an ancient biblical lament. These writings are prayers, cries to God, requesting an end to suffering. Laments have two essential elements: petitions and praise. They may begin negative, but they don't stay there, they always end on a positive note.

In today's psalm, David feels that the Lord has forgotten him in his time of great need. He wants to know, how much longer God is going to leave him here. How long must he continue to suffer? Have you ever been there? Like a sitting duck you sit in your mess, your pit, your despair, waiting for the Lord to rescue you, save you, pull you out? I can recall a time when I could identify with David's pain. After a serious car accident, I was left with immobilizing knee pain that grew progressively worse instead of better. The doctors gave a new meaning to the term "practicing medicine" as they struggled to diagnose my problem. In the meantime, the pain worsened and so did my lack of mobility. Days turned to weeks, weeks to months... I cried out to God in desperation... When are you going to fix this God? It seemed that God had hidden his face from me (vs. 1). When God hides His face from those who depend on Him, we are left in despair. But when He shines His face on us, blessings and deliverance are forthcoming. What do you need God to shine His face on today? A persistent illness? A lost family member? A career heading in the wrong direction? Psalm 13 teaches us that in the midst of our trials, we are to praise God.

Even in the midst of his despair, David commits to TRUST in God's unfailing love, REJOICE in the Lord's salvation (vs. 5, emphasis mine) and SING to God... Why? Because as bad as the situation may seem, God has STILL been good to him. My brother and sister, despite your current situation, God has still been good to you and therefore He is worthy of your praise! Praise isn't based on your feelings or your present reality... It is given to God for who He is... Who is God to you? Even before my leg was healed, God was my Jehovah Rapha (the Lord my healer) because that is who He promised to be. Who has God promised to be to you in the midst of the situation you face today?

Psalm 14

Lets face it; things are less than ideal in our world. Crime, poverty, greed, and hatred abound. We are plagued with the persisting sins of racism, sexism, and classism. Children are dropping like flies in urban communities as a result of gun violence. Our economy is in the toilet, which only exasperates and increases homelessness, lawlessness, and stimulates feelings of desperation.

In this Psalm of David, the writer laments about the evil doers/wicked that abound. They are not only plentiful, but seem to have success with their immoral schemes. They are corrupt and their deeds are vile (vs. 1), which rings true of our fools/wrongdoers today. Whether we are looking at the modern day wicked or those of old, they have much in common, particularly in their persistence in evildoing and disregard of God and His standards.

David hit the nail on the head when he identified the source of their problem as one of the heart. Proverbs 4:23 says that it is the wellspring of life. Matthew 6:21 says "Where your treasure is, there your heart will be also." These individuals lack purity of heart (i.e. hearts surrendered to God) Verse 1 of this text says that they say in their heart that there is no God. If God is not in your heart then you are doomed to live a life outside of His will. Without God at the center of your heart, He is not centrally positioned in your life either; your actions flow from your flesh. The flesh does what it wants, when it wants, and how it wants if left unchecked by God and His Word. Flesh over consumes food and alcohol, lacks the motivation to seek the fulfillment of divine purpose, disrespects the temples of others, and sees God's creatures and creation as means to the achieve personal gain. Without God, we are left to a life of foolishness and sin.

David was sick of it and made the most productive choice, he took his frustration to God. He realized that as bad as things were that God was still on the throne. What social issue do you need to lay at Gods feet today? Poverty? Abortion? Homosexuality? Racism? Governmental corruption? Trust God to bring restoration in your life, community, nation, and world, just as the writer of Psalm 14. God can and will do it!

Psalm 15

The psalmist begins this prayer with a question, who can dwell in the tabernacle of God? As I read God's response to this weighty question, I had my own question--who in the world could live up to His standard? Blameless walk, speaks no slander, doesn't hurt neighbors, keeps oaths at all costs, and the list drags on and on with higher and higher standards.

As I read on, I heard the Holy Spirit whisper a response to my question, "Jesus." Jesus is the only one who can live up to this standard. He is the only one who deserves to dwell in the house of God. Leviticus 20:7 commands us to, "Consecrate yourselves and be holy, because I am the Lord your God." Isaiah 6:3 says "One cried to another and said, Holy, holy, holy is the Lord of hosts; the whole earth is full of His glory!" Our God is holy. He is without sin, without fault and above reproach. Therefore, those who dwell, tabernacle, stay in the place where God's spirit resides must be holy as well. In order to stay in God's presence we must conduct our lives in a manner fitting of the one who we come to worship. Jesus was the only one who could do it. 1 Peter 2:22 says that "He committed no sin and no deceit was in his mouth." Jesus is the only one who deserves to dwell.

Thank God for Jesus Christ. As a result of His life, death, burial, and resurrection, we receive benefits and privileges that we do not deserve (Galatians 1:4, 1 Peter 2:24, 1 John 4:10). God graciously extends Christ's reward to us. We receive eternal love from and intimacy with God. "For I am convinced that neither death nor life, neither angels nor demons, neither the present nor the future, nor any powers, neither height nor depth, nor anything else in all creation, will be able to separate us from the love of God that is in Christ Jesus our Lord" (Romans 8:38-39). There is nothing that we have to do to earn the love of God we already have it. God simply asks that we obey His commands and remain faithful to Him. "Remain in me, as I also remain in you. No branch can bear fruit by itself; it must remain in the vine. Neither can you bear fruit unless you remain in me" (John 15:4).

Although we do not deserve to stand in God's presence, to worship in His holy temple, or receive His love, Jesus created a clear pathway for us to do so. Thank God for Jesus today! For His blameless life and sacrifice that allows you to dwell in the presence and in the house of the Lord all the days of your life.

Psalm 16

In this Prayer for Safekeeping, David begins by simply laying his petition before the Lord; "Keep me safe, O God" (vs. 1). He doesn't pray anything deep or heavy. He doesn't make an eloquent theological statement or offer God any moving poetic words. Like a daughter frustrated with her math homework or a son that can't reach the cookie jar, David went to his Father and said, "help me!!!" Why do we make our prayer lives so complicated? Why do we feel the need to fill it with words that we wouldn't use outside of the church to attempt to communicate with God? When was the last time you used the word thou in conversation with a co-worker? What about thine? Hath? Thy or shall? Rarely, right? Because we don't speak the king's English!!!

Reading this psalm reminded me of the need for us to be authentic in our prayer lives. If it isn't real, it doesn't count. Prayer is our primary method of communication with God. It is meant to be a conversation. In the same way that we talk to our friends, family members, and co-workers to maintain a relationship with them, we should do so with God. How would you feel if one of those people pretended to be someone that they were not? That is exactly what we are doing when we come to God unauthentically.

It is time to become transparent in your prayer life. If you need help, ask for just that—help! Do not beat around the bush. "Don't bargain with God. Be direct. Ask for what you need. This isn't a cat-and-mouse, hide-and-seek game we're in. If your child asks for bread, do you trick him with sawdust? If he asks for fish, do you scare him with a live snake on his plate? As bad as you are, you wouldn't think of such a thing. You're at least decent to your own children. So don't you think the God who conceived you in love will be even better?" (Matthew 7:7-11, Message Bible).

Ask God for what you need and then start praising Him. That is what David did in this psalm. He spent verse 1 asking for safekeeping and the remaining ten verses declaring his trust in God and in His faithfulness. The writer believed in God and

God's unmatched track record of responding to his prayers and meeting his needs. David simply prayed and moved on as if God had answered the prayer. David put Romans 4:17 into practice; he called those things into existence as if they already were so.

What do you need to ask God for and then praise God for, even before you can see the manifestation? Do it, today!

Psalm 17

Today, we meet David once again in the midst of prayer time. It seems he was always on his knees; going before God to pour out his heart. This time, he petitions God as judge. God is not one dimensional, but has more depth to His character than anyone who has ever walked this earth (other than Jesus and Jesus and the Father are one). Not only is God our king, our father, our mother, our healer, our deliverer, our way maker, and our provider, He is also our JUDGE. Judges are responsible for ensuring that laws are followed in cases where a jury is present. She doesn't try to prove one guilty or innocent, but remains impartial. When there is no jury, the judge is the fact finder. She listens to the evidence without passing judgment until all sides are heard and then renders a decision. As our judge, God is more like the latter. He has ultimate authority. Sovereign authority. Sole authority. David appeals to God for justice, because his enemies are getting the best of him and he is fed up.

How are we to respond when we are tired of a situation? When we have come to the end of our rope? The psalm writer shows us in verse 2 when he prayed, "may my vindication come from you, may your eyes see what is right." Our defense comes from God. Period. Not from our parents, friends, spouses, co-workers, the government, or even ourselves. Vindication comes from God. How many times do we feel the need to vindicate ourselves? We attempt to explain situations, change the minds of others, and prove ourselves innocent or worthy. As the apple of God's eye (vs.8), we are hidden from our enemies under the shadow of God's wing (vs. 8). Let me ask you, when was the last time you hid someone under your wing? When was the last time that someone protected you from hurt, harm, or danger? Do human beings have the ability to protect one another? No, not really. Only God can take care of us, therefore that is where we should place our trust and hope.

Pray with me: *God vindicate your people. Bring us justice. Provide a way of escape for us. Until that time, help us to trust in you and you alone. Keep our feet from slipping, our minds from straying, and our hearts from fainting. We desire to please you. We trust in you and know that no matter what comes our way you will see us through. In Jesus name, Amen.*

Psalm 18

A testimony is truly one of the most powerful and effective witnessing tools. Hearing what the Lord has done for another can serve as a source of encouragement, hope, and strength. It can also help to educate someone about God and His nature. A testimony plants seeds in the heart of one person, softens the soil in the heart of another, and uproots weeds that had grown wild in yet another heart. A testimony tells the story of how an individual was faced with a test and how they overcame. Psalm 18 is a real account of how God brought David through the reoccurring test of facing enemies on every side. The writer provides a wonderful model for how we, as believers, can share our testimony with others.

He begins with a statement of affection and a proclamation of who God has revealed himself to be during his trial. After expressing love for the Lord, David calls God his strength, rock, fortress, the one in whom he takes refuge, his shield, the horn of his salvation and his stronghold (vs. 1-2). During times of adversity, if we cling to God, we will learn new things about God and His nature. Times of adversity are a great time to "get to know God" better. If God responds to our cries from the bottom of a pit, we discover that God hears the cry of His people. If we are scared and run to God in prayer and worship, we discover that God is a refuge for those who run to Him. If God heals our broken heart, we discover that God is the one who mends our broken lives. Yes, hard times are the best time to learn more about the One we serve. Who has God revealed Himself to be during your test or trial?

Next, David gives us a blow-by-blow encounter of EXACTLY how God brought him through his time of testing. Can't you see it? David paints a vivid picture of exactly how God responded to his cry for help. There was an earthquake, smoke, hail, lighting, and so much more when God came down from heaven to see about His child. How did the atmosphere of your life shift when God delivered you from your enemies, from your sickness, from your poverty, from distress, from yourself? It is so very important that we not only remember, but that we share with others how God operates in our lives. Did He turn your mourning into dancing? (Psalm 30:11) Did He turn your darkness into light (Job 12:22)? When God shows up, something shifts in the atmosphere, in our world, and in our lives. What type of shift did you experience?

Finally, David ends the psalm with a beautiful hymn of praise. Based on what you have learned about God during your test, what would YOUR hymn of praise sound like? What would you want others to know about YOUR God and YOUR God's abilities? What are the "who," "what," "when," "where," and "how" of your deliverance? I encourage you to take a moment to brag on your God by writing a hymn of praise. After God delivered David, David believed that he could "stand on the heights" (vs. 33), and "bend a bow of bronze" (vs. 34). Yes, you too can do all things through Christ that give you strength (Philippians 4:13). You know that about God because Paul shared his testimony with you. What does the world need to know about God through your testimony?

Psalm 19

What role does the Word of God play in your life? Does it hold a position of reverence or is it just another collection of books and stories? Do you read it as truth or peruse it with skepticism? Is it a guiding light for your life or simply filled with suggestions? These are the types of questions that arise within me each time I read this Psalm of David. Regardless of the subjective decisions we make regarding the placement of the scriptures in our lives, the Word of God is, what it is...

- **Perfect**
- **Trustworthy**
- **Right**
- **Radiant**
- **Pure**
- **Endures Forever**
- **Sure**
- **Righteous**
- **Precious**
- **Sweet**

It is up to us to allow them to:

- **Revive the soul**
- **Make us wise**
- **Give joy to our heart**
- **Bring light to our eyes**
- **Warn us**
- **Reap a great reward**

When the Word of God holds a place of reverence in our lives we read the Bible regularly, coming to it with an open heart, mind, and soul. In so doing, we are able to hear from the Holy Spirit as to how these words of truth are to guide us, lead us, and direct us in our present season. The Word is perfect, trustworthy, right, radiant, pure, enduring, sure, righteous, precious, and sweet. It is up to us to allow God's Word to permeate our beings and transform our world.

Will you allow the Word of God to change you today? Do you desire to receive the rewards that David mentioned in today's psalm? If so, commit to submit to the move of the Holy Spirit in your life through obedience to God's Word. You have nothing to lose, but much to gain.

Psalm 20

This psalm is a Prayer of Intercession, offered to God on behalf of the king prior to battle. Intercession is an act of love. We are called to love our neighbor as ourselves (Mark 12:31). I cannot think of a more loving act than someone praying for me. When I am sick, in distress, financially strapped, or seeking revelation from God, to know that someone is praying for me is encouraging. To go to God on behalf of another, requires someone to lay down his or her own needs, and take on those of another. Instead of talking to God about what you need, you are taking time to petition heaven for your brother or sister.

Although we, as Christians, have the ability to petition God individually, God wants us to pray for one another. "Is anyone among you in trouble? Let them pray. Is anyone happy? Let them sing songs of praise" (James 5:13); "Confess your sins to each other and pray for each other so that you may be healed. The prayer of a righteous person is powerful and effective. (James 5:16); "Pray in the Spirit on all occasions with all kinds of prayers and requests. With this in mind, be alert and always keep on praying for all the Lord's people" (Ephesians 6:18). Prayer not only connects us to God, but it also connects us to one another. Through prayer, I become concerned with you and you also with me.

My favorite part of this prayer of intercession was not when the writer asked for protection for the king (vs.1) or when he/she asked for God to provide him with the desires of his heart (vs. 4), but it is found in verse 7. After the writer petitions God to protect the king during this rigorous battle, he makes a powerful declaration; "Some trust in chariots and some in horses, but we trust in the name of the Lord our God." The writer declares trust in God for himself, the king, and the army above all else. Often times, we rely on individuals and institutions and not God. We become dependent on our jobs to provide for us, our doctors to heal us, our lawyers to justify us, and our family members to care for us, but such trust in misguided. We are to trust God above everyone and everything else. The writer is clear that WHEN this army receives the victory over their enemies it will

36

not be the result of excellent fighting men, or superior equipment, but as a result of the divine protection of God.

Where is your trust today? Who or what are you looking to bring you out or through a situation? What is your chariot or horse, today?

Make the decision to trust in the Lord above all else!

Psalm 21

In our psalm today, the people rejoice and give God praise for blessing the king and answering his prayer. They go on and on recalling how the Lord caused the king to be victorious in battle. The writer's love for the king is evident by the praise given to God for granting him the "desires of his heart" (vs. 2). The ability to pray for someone, with sincerity of heart, is an act of love. Most of us will pray for the needs and concerns of others, but can we praise God for blessing them? For answering their prayers? For giving them the desires of their heart?

Let me be clear, I am not talking about a pity pat praise. Instead I am referring to a Psalm 21 kind of praise. The writer recalls the way that God blessed the king with great detail. He praises God for everything from the crown he placed on his head to the glory, splendor, and majesty bestowed upon him (vs. 3-7). When we love our neighbor as ourselves, we praise God when they are victorious with the same fervor, vigor, and sincerity that we would if God had bestowed those blessings upon us.

What has God done in the life of your loved ones that you need to praise Him for? Has He healed your mother? Saved your sister? Delivered your father? Provided for your sister? If so, you need to give God the praise that He is due. "Sing to him, sing praise to him; tell of all his wonderful acts" (1 Chronicles 16:9). "Give thanks to the Lord, for he is good; his love endures forever" (1 Chronicles 16:34).

There is one prerequisite to praising God for blessing your neighbor—you must be sincerely "happy" for them. You can hear that the writer of Psalm 21 is overjoyed for the king. Jealousy, envy, covetousness, and competition will prevent you from truly celebrating another person and the move of God in their life. In James chapters 3 and 4, we are repeatedly cautioned against jealousy, bitterness, covetousness, and other spirits that cause us to compare ourselves to our neighbors. Doing so is not only sinful, but also counterproductive. God has a specific plan for your life to prosper you (Jeremiah 29:11), which is greater than anything you can even ask for or imagine (Ephesians 3:20). Since God's ways are higher than ours (Isaiah 55:8), why would you spend your time thirsting for something that is second rate? Nothing that you can think up for yourself can compare to the higher way/higher plan that God has for your life. Let go and let God. Allow the move of God in your neighbor's life to encourage you and minister to you about how God can move in your life. Celebrate your brother and sister wholeheartedly; and they will celebrate with you.

Pray with me: *God, help me to celebrate the blessings in the lives of those around me. Help me to support them, applaud them, and rejoice for them, in your name. Give me the strength to lay down my selfish desires, dreams, and goals long enough to regard my neighbor fondly. I praise you for what you are doing in their lives and believe you to move in mine. In Jesus name, Amen.*

Psalm 22

Have you ever felt forsaken? Abandoned? Renounced? Left behind? Do you feel like that today? If so, you are not alone. One of the biggest tricks of the enemy is to cause us to feel as if we have been left alone on a deserted island, like you are the only person in human history to be forsaken, that no one cares about us, and no one will come after us. Remember: the devil is a liar and the father of lies (John 8:44), so this is a tactic, a trick of the enemy. Job felt forsaken; "Why do you hide your face and consider me your enemy?" (Job 13:24) The writer of this psalm (David) felt forsaken; look at verse 1, "my God, my God, why have you forsaken me?" Jesus also felt forsaken and cried out the same words of David "my God, my God, why have you forsaken me?" (Matthew 27:46). I too have felt forsaken. I urge you to resist the bait of the enemy when he tells you that you are the first and only person to feel abandoned, alone, and renounced by God.

After voicing his lament to God in verses 1 and 2, the writer recalled what God had been to His people in the past. I encourage you to follow the psalm writer's lead. Think back. Who has God been to you in the past? Healer? Deliverer? Provider? Friend? Protector? David recalled how God was one who could be trusted (vs. 4), the deliverer of His people (vs. 4), an open ear to the cry of the people of Israel (vs. 5), and was a reliable savior (vs. 5). Again I ask, who has God been to you? Your family? Your people? Your generation? When we are in despair, particularly when we feel forsaken, it is helpful to rehearse who God has been to us and our loved ones in the past, because we are reminded of God's character. God promised in Deuteronomy 3:16 to never leave us nor forsake us. So when we remind ourselves of who God has been, the lies of the enemy have no choice but to be exposed. Satan's words will always be contrary to the Word of God and God's nature.

Although David continued his lament for thirteen more verse, he eventually found his way out of anguish and freed himself from the lies of the enemy. He spends the rest of this psalm professing His trust in God. Although the writer began his time with the Lord feeling forsaken, he came to realize that the Lord was not far off (vs. 19) and trusted in God to help (vs. 19), deliver (vs. 20), rescue (vs. 21), and save him (vs. 21). Get specific with God today. What EXACTLY is it that you need God to do for you?

Now praise God in advance! Although the move of God may not be apparent yet, praise the Lord as if it has already been seen. David declared, "I will declare your name to my brothers; in the congregation I will praise you" (vs. 22). It is time to praise God in advance for your breakthrough, healing, deliverance, and change—despite how you may feel!

Psalm 23

Considering the feelings of forsakenness we discussed yesterday, Psalm 23 is a great successor. If you are unsure how to profess trust in the Lord in the midst of unfavorable circumstances, this scripture is a great place to start. In this text, David proclaims joyful trust in God as his shepherd and king. Since David was a shepherd until he was called to serve Saul, he knew the qualifications of a good shepherd and recognized God as such.

Since God is such a great shepherd, we do not have to want for anything (vs. 1). There is no need for us to want because, "God will meet all your needs according to the riches of his glory in Christ Jesus" (Philippians 4:19). "Look at the birds of the air; they do not sow or reap or store away in barns, and yet your heavenly Father feeds them. Are you not much more valuable than they?" (Matthew 6:26). Nope, there is nothing for us to worry about because God takes care of every need we could possibly have. Since all of our needs are met, we can find contentment and security and rest in peace (vs. 2). If your problems are keeping you up at night I encourage you to consider whether you have fully relinquished them to "The Shepherd" to handle them. If not, let them go. You cannot hold on to your problems and give them to God at the same time! Make a choice.

As our shepherd, God guides us down the safe path (vs. 3). Our God leads us down the roads of prosperity and security. Wherever God instructs you to go, will lead to the best destination for you. Do you trust that? Do you believe that? Although God gives humans the freewill to make choices, the choice to follow God is ultimately the best choice one could make. Why? Because God's plans are for our good. "For I know the plans I have for you," declares the Lord, "plans to prosper you and not to harm you, plans to give you hope and a future" (Jeremiah 29:11). In this dark and sad world, don't you desire plans of hope and a future? Follow God.

Even when the path that God chooses for you gets hard, God will be there to comfort you with His rod and staff (vs. 4). There is nothing to fear. As a shepherd uses his rod to protect his sheep from wolves and other dangerous predators, God too will protect you. "But the Lord is faithful. He will establish you and guard you against the evil one" (2 Thessalonians 3:3) If people talk about you, God will be there. If systems attempt to oppress you, God will be there. If the enemy attacks, God will be there. No matter what you encounter, God will be your banner and protect you from dangers seen and unseen. He will support and comfort you with His loving staff. Just as God sent His son Jesus to save you (and the entire world) over 2000 years ago, He will use His staff TODAY to comfort you when you hurt, when you are afraid, and when you grieve.

The Lord is your shepherd. Trust that! Believe that! Declare that!

Pray with me: *Lord, help me to know you as the good shepherd today. Manifest yourself as a provider, protector, comforter, guide, healer, and friend today. In Jesus name, Amen.*

Psalm 24

It is often easy to forget that we do not own anything. Everything is Gods! In this Psalm of David, it is declared that the "earth is the Lord's and everything in it." (vs. 1). God founded and established the earth and everything in it, (vs. 2) which means that God owns everything on the planet, including every person, place, and thing. God alone is the mastermind behind all of creation. I do not own myself and neither do you. As owner of humanity, God has the sole right of possession and control. He can do what He desires with us and allow anything to happen to us that He chooses. Our lives are solely left to the plan and purposes of God. Jeremiah 29:11 says that God knows the plans He has for each of our lives. The day that we let go of the misnomer that we control ourselves and have a right to ourselves will be the day that we enter the flow of the spirit of God. Say it with me, "God is in control of me and everything He created."

To surrender to God's control is to bow to His sovereignty over us. One who is sovereign is:

- **Supreme in authority**
- **Ruler**
- **Self-governing**
- **Independent**
- **Unmitigated**

As the controller of creation, God does not need permission to act. God has the right and ability to do whatever He chooses at any and all times. He can wake you up tomorrow morning or not. He can relocate you to Greenland or India. He can bless you with a beautiful spouse and children or allow you to never marry or conceive. He can keep hurt, harm, and danger from showing up at your door or offer you up as He did Job. God is a sovereign ruler who in control and owner of all. "For it is God who works in you to will and to act in order to fulfill his good purpose." (Philippians 2:13). It is the will of God that allows, keeps, blesses, and prevents. Fortunately, our God is gracious and merciful. He gives us things that we don't deserve and does not hand down every punishment that we do deserve.

If you are struggling with the circumstances of your life, I encourage you to remember that the "earth is the Lord's and everything in it." (vs. 1) God is in control of you, your circumstance, and everything concerning you. If He was able to establish the earth on the waters, He can definitely take care of whatever situation concerns you today. The same way that God controls and owns you...He also owns and control every person, place, and thing that you could ever encounter. Be encouraged today; God is still on the throne!

Psalm 25

I was overwhelmed as I read this Psalm of David today. Although this is a prayer for the mercy of God during times of trouble and difficulty, I saw past the hurt and disappointment of the writer and found encouragement. As I read through the verses, numerous promises of God jumped out at me. I could hear the spirit of God saying "in the depths of despair, at the bottom of your pit and when all hope seems lost to rehearse the promises of God." Say them out loud, over and over again. Meditate on them. Pray them. Declare them. Until you believe them!

A friend of mine has a saying, "fake it until you make it!" That phrase has blessed me tremendously during times of adversity, especially when God seemed distant. I read, write, recite, and declare the promises of God until I either believe them or they manifest before my eyes. David must have known my mentor, because he seemed to be faking it until he made it. As I read this psalm, I didn't hear fear, concern, weariness or doubt, but instead certainty of who God is, how God would manifest himself, and what God would do for David.

Look at all the promises of God that David recited in this psalm:
- **Shame-free living**
- **Shame-filled living for the treacherous**
- **Guidance**
- **Instruction in God's ways**
- **Love and faithfulness**
- **Revelation about God's plan**
- **Prosperity**
- **Inheritance for our descendants**
- **Trust in us**
- **Revelation**
- **Deliverance**

Hopefully it is clear to you why David didn't "look like" or "sound like" what he was going through after reading all of these promises. David knew that he served a God that was everything that he needed to make it through his current trial.

What has God promised you? Refer back to that promise. Allow it to encourage you and sustain you in times of adversity. Write it down, again! Pray it. Recite it. Share it with someone else. "Know therefore that the Lord your God is God; he is the faithful God, keeping his covenant of love to a thousand generations of those who love him and keep his commandments" (Deuteronomy 7:9). God will NOT fail you!

Psalm 26

How are you living? As David cries out to the Lord for vindication in this psalm, he does not come empty-handed. He appeals to God based on his moral integrity, unwavering trust in God, and his sincere satisfaction in the Lord. David reminds God that he has lived a blameless life and trusted God without wavering (vs. 1). He does not dwell with the ungodly, but hates evil (vs. 4-5). He lives a life of praise and evangelism (vs. 7). David continues his moral laundry list throughout the psalm, sharing with God all of the things that he has done to try to please God. What about you? What do the pages of your life look like? Do they reflect a life lived with moral integrity or hypocrisy? Are they pages full of stories of your trust in God or a life lived apart from God? Can you, like David, take the pages of your life to God as support for your requests?

When David speaks of a "blameless" life, he is not referring to perfection. None of us are perfect or capable of perfection — we are sinners. The Word of God teaches us that: "all have sinned and fall short of the glory of God" (Romans 3:23) and "there is no one righteous, not even one" (Romans 3:10). The only one that was, is, and who will ever be perfect is Jesus Christ (2 Corinthians 5:21). So what in the world was David talking about when he repeatedly referred to himself as "blameless." Blamelessness is godliness. This is a life characterized by trust and obedience in God and the Word of God. David was making a claim of both moral integrity and faithfulness. Are you faithful? Do you trust in God? Are you obedient to the Word and the will of God?

As a result of his godliness, David could go before the Lord with confidence that his life, prayers, and desires were within the will of God. When we are obedient to God, we can go to God with full confidence that we will be in the will of God, no matter the outcome of our situation. When we are obedient we can trust God. "Trust in the Lord with all your heart, and do not lean on your own understanding. In all your ways acknowledge Him, and He will make your paths straight" (Proverbs 3:5-6). By obeying God's will, we can be confident that our enemies will be silenced. "For it is God's will that by doing good you should silence the ignorant talk of foolish people" (1 Peter 2:15). When we walk in God's will, we can be confident that we will receive the promises of God. "So do not throw away your confidence; it will be richly rewarded. You need to persevere so that when you have done the will of God, you will receive what he has promised" (Hebrews 10:35-36).

Commit to lead a blameless life, no matter the circumstance. Commit to obey God, trust God, to be faithful to God and the Word. It is worth it!

Psalm 27

I like to call this an Encourage Yourself Psalm. Commentators believe that David wrote this psalm when he was exiled and running from King Saul. Verse 2 substantiates that at a minimum, he was concerned about the advances of the wicked and besiegement of a great army. Whether running from the highest-ranking official in the land or a vast army, David had reasoned to be afraid, flustered, and low-spirited. However, he made a choice, the choice to "fake it." He chose to speak those things that were not, as if they already were. He spoke life, although death could be imminent (vs. 13). He spoke trust, although doubt may have been brewing within (vs. 4-5). He spoke patience, although he needed a prompt move of God (vs. 14). He spoke protection, although he may have felt abandoned (vs. 10). David made bold and audacious declarations before the Lord, in the midst of a persistent trial.

David not only petitioned the Lord in this text, but also commanded himself to place his trust in the Lord. The result of which, was a lifting of his spirits. This psalm is framed by declarations of trust. In verse 1, David professes that God is his light, salvation, and the stronghold of his life—God is his fortress. While being pursued by a great army, the Great Fortress is exactly what he needed. David moves on to state that God will keep him safe and hide him when trouble comes. I am sure that David dreaded the day that his enemies would find him. Instead of allowing himself to be overtaken by this concern, he professed confidence that the Lord would not only keep him safe, but beyond the reach of his enemies (vs. 5-6). Again in verse 10, David professes that even if everyone abandons him that he will not be alone, because the Lord will welcome him. He concludes this framework of trust in verse 13 by boldly stating that he will "remain confident," despite everything that is happening within and around him.

What is the framework of your speech during times of adversity? Particularly when you are under attack from your enemies? What we speak is very important; "the tongue has the power of life and death, and those who love it will eat its fruit" (Proverbs 18:21). Not only because what we speak influences what comes to us, but more importantly it impacts what happens within us. We eat what we speak. That means we literally chew on, think on, and meditate on what we profess. Long before we act, there were words spoken, thoughts meditated on, and emotions felt. Choosing to profess trust in the Lord places a roadblock in the path of doubtful thoughts, and fear filled emotions.

If deliverance, protection, help, confidence, comfort, and support is what you need to experience during times of difficulty began to speak that, despite what you feel or see. Why? Because God is able to do "immeasurably more than all we ask or imagine, according to his power that is at work within us" (Ephesians 3:20). David knew this truth and encouraged himself as he placed his trust in the Lord. Trust God, today.

Psalm 28

As I read this psalm, I was reminded of how intimately acquainted David was with the Word of God. Although we know that he was an imperfect man, king, husband and father, God referred to him as man after His heart (1 Samuel 13:14). Much ink has been spilled opining and attempting to exegete the meaning of this statement. Despite where one comes out on the significance of God's statement about David, we get a glimpse into the role that scripture plays in David's life in Psalm 28. He not only knew it, but he believed it. Instead of personally unleashing his wrath on his enemies, David consistently turned the fate of his enemies over to God. Leviticus 19:18 states that "you shall not take vengeance or bear a grudge against the sons of your own people, but you shall love your neighbor as yourself: I am the Lord."

I often read some of this writer's prayers about his enemies and am astonished. I think to myself "did he really say that?" "Did he really ask God for that?" David had no problem requesting that God would punish his enemies; that seems a bit harsh, doesn't it? Which one is worse, for you to go after your enemies (in your own strength) or for you to talk to God about your feelings and ask Him to handle it? The Bible teaches us to cast our cares on God, because He not only can handle it, but because He cares for us (1 Peter 5:7). Taking the issue to God expresses trust in God. By so doing, you are saying "here is what's going on with me God, handle it." Since there is nothing that can separate us from the love of God, there is nothing that you can express to God that will adversely effect His love for you. Telling God your feelings, problems, and concerns is always best! My mother used to tell me that telling her, even when I acted improperly, was always the best choice, because in so doing she could help me, advise me, and even protect me. How much more can God do for you?

Asking God to handle your enemies also expresses dependence on God. When we pray, and truly leave our requests with God we are surrendering to His sovereign will. We are literally praying, Matthew 6:10 "thy will be done" over our lives. Remember, we can't hold onto something and give it to God at the same time. When we give it to God, we are saying that "your way is better than mine, despite what I may want; God you know best." This is one of the greatest acts of "loving our neighbors as ourselves." Would you rather be left to the whims of humans or God? I pick God everyday. Why? Because God is merciful and gracious, <u>ALL THE TIME</u> and humans are not. Mercy and grace are parts of God's character, so He does not have to work at being merciful and gracious, but humans express grace and mercy only when we allow the spirit of God to overcome our fleshly propensities. When I harm my neighbor, I want God to handle me. When I speak words I shouldn't, I want God to handle me. When I act of out of selfish ambition, I want God to handle me. NOT the one whom my actions hurt. "The Lord is gracious and compassionate, slow to anger and rich in love" (Psalm 145:8). People, not so much! Turn it over to God today.

Psalm 29

What is it that you know to be true about God? What characteristics do you attribute to the Lord? Today, David implores us to tell everyone about whom God has manifested Himself to be in our lives. He begins by attributing glory, strength, splendor, and holiness to God (vs. 1 and 2). Declarations about the character of God are a form of praise and hence are not dependent on our emotions, the status of our lives, or our perceived wellbeing. Psalm 96:4 declares that "Great is the Lord and most worthy of praise; He is to be feared above all gods." Note, that this is a fact; God IS great. Period. God IS to be feared above all our little gods. Little gods? Yes, above our other relationships, possessions, tasks, desires, needs, and our flesh. Since God IS great and to be feared, He IS most worthy of our praise. David was able to ascribe to the Lord great character, even in the midst of his darkest hour, because he knew and accepted that God IS…

Have you made up in your mind that God IS great? Despite what you're going through in this season; do you believe that God is still on the throne? As long as God is still God and is still great and is still on the throne, He is worthy of your praise. Make a conscious decision to shift beyond your sadness, sickness, frustration, disappointment, financial situation, relationship status, and whatever else you deem imperfect with your life and give the Lord praise.

In Psalm 29, David chose to focus on the voice of the Lord. He went into great detail to describe the reach, strength, ability, and impact of God's voice. It was described as reigning and mighty (vs. 3), powerful and majestic (vs. 4), possessing the ability to break (vs. 5), leap (vs. 6), strike (vs. 7), shake (vs. 8) and twist (vs. 9). This praise comes from a place of awe and wonder within David. What characteristic of God causes excitement and amazement within you? Describe it. Write about it. Talk about it. Is it the hand of God? The heart of God? The eyes of God?

"Ascribe to the Lord the glory due his name; worship the Lord in the splendor of his holiness" (vs. 2) because our God IS!!!

Psalm 30

In this Song of David, we have the privilege of hearing a testimony. This psalm encouraged my heart. In light of all the trials, tribulations, and tests that we read about in the past 29 Psalms, it is good to see a testimony. A testimony is good news because it means that David made it to the other side of the test. There is not a testimony without a test, and there isn't a testimony until the test is over. A testimony is a declaration by a witness; a public declaration about a religious experience; and evidence of support of a fact or assertion. A testimony is proof. Here, David gives proof that God IS...

Be encouraged today by David's testimony. David asked God for help and He healed him. God spared his life and restored his joy. Whatever you are believing God for, don't give up. "Let us not become weary in doing good, for at the proper time we will reap a harvest if we do not give up" (Galatians 6:9). In this psalm, David talks about his healing, how God restored him from his deathbed. We also know that David had to deal with attacks on his life, abandonment, haters, and so much more (recall what you read in Psalm 1-29). David went through a lot, but we also know that God answered his cry for help, because he sang his testimony in this song.

What has God already done for you? What has He already brought you through? What way did He make for you in the past? Write about it. Sing about it. Talk about it. You might find that your recollection of your test and deliverance will not only bless someone else, but you as well. I believe that writing this song increased David's faith and filled him with encouragement. When we tell of the goodness of God, we are able to remember how great God is and all the wonderful things He has done. Your testimony is full proof! It is 100% authentic. It includes both a problem and a solution. It is also the best story there is; it includes a: who, what, when, where, why, and how. And my favorite part about testimonies is that they are factual. Your testimony is a fact about you and about God. Give witness to God, so that you and others can praise God and trust Him more.

Psalm 31

Today, David prays for deliverance from conspiracy. Enemies set traps for him (vs. 4), friends abandoned him (vs. 11-12), foes were trying to kill him (vs. 13), and he was being slandered (vs. 13). He was going through and cried out to the Lord. From verses 9 to 18 he prayed fervently for mercy in the midst of his suffering. Notice that David prayed for mercy and not grace. Mercy is God withholding what we deserve and grace is God bestowing upon us what we don't deserve. David humbly recognized that he was unworthy, for whatever reason, of the deliverance of God, but he trusted God anyway. Why do you think David felt that he did not deserve the Lord's help? I believe it was due to his sin and his flaws. Think back over the words of David that we have read in previous psalms, he was painfully aware of his imperfections and keenly aware of God's perfection.

In the midst of everything that was going on, David laid his case and life in the hands of God. In verse 5 he declared, "Into your hands I commit my spirit." This statement was the ultimate expression of trust in God. In the midst of his suffering, David decided to trust God to protect and deliver him. Instead of relying on himself, other humans, or even the weapons of a vast army, David made the conscious choice to believe God. The words of David in verse 5 were echoed by Jesus in Luke 23:46. Like David, Jesus was suffering. He too was being persecuted, had been abandoned by friends, followers and loved ones, and was in the midst of the biggest conspiracy in human history. Jesus spoke these words, as He died on the cross. Jesus identified with the feelings of hurt and disappointment that David expressed in Psalm 31. But there is one significant difference between the circumstance surrounding David's declaration and Jesus'—Jesus was completely innocent. "He committed no sin, and no deceit was found in his mouth" (1 Peter 2:22). Jesus, as the Son of God, was perfect. Yet He identified with the human devastation of David.

As you pray your way and fight your way through the tests and trials of life, be encouraged. "Therefore, since we have a great high priest who has ascended into heaven, Jesus the Son of God, let us hold firmly to the faith we profess. For we do not have a high priest who is unable to empathize with our weaknesses, but we have one who has been tempted in every way, just as we are—yet he did not sin. Let us then approach God's throne of grace with confidence, so that we may receive mercy and find grace to help us in our time of need." (Hebrews 4:14-18) Jesus knows exactly how you feel. Trust God with whatever you are going through. Trust Him enough to deposit your circumstance into His mighty hands. Allow your spirit to agree with both David and Jesus. Say to God today, as you release your concern and your life--"into your hands I commit my spirit."

Psalm 32

Why is it so difficult for us to confess our sin? Is it that we are so arrogant that we don't truly believe we have sinned? Is that that we feel ashamed of our shortcomings? Is it that sin flows so naturally from our beings that we don't realize that we have sinned? Is it that we don't know how to own up to the things we've done? I believe it is all of these reasons and a myriad of others. Whatever our reason for failing to confess, David makes clear in Psalm 32 that we are missing out by doing so.

What are we missing out on? Forgiveness. Blessedness. Peace. Instruction. Ultimately, we are missing out on intimacy with God. There is no trick or gimmick; if we confess our wrongdoing to God, He will forgive us (vs. 5). We find yet another wonderful promise of God in this psalm...forgiveness. The only thing keeping us from tapping into this forgiveness is our inability to confess our sins. Get out of your own way, Leah, open up your mouth and admit to God what you have done wrong. God is so gracious that He does not require us to confess our sins to one another to receive His forgiveness. This is why David implores us to seek God through prayer, tell the Lord about our faults, and be delivered from the guilt and shame of sin.

How is failing to confess your sin working for you? Really? Are your sins haunting you through flashbacks, memories, and sleepless nights? Do you feel anxiety, stress, guilt, or shame? There is good news in Psalm 32, you can be delivered. David was killing himself and groaning daily as a result of his unrepentant posture. He felt the weight of his sin. But when David confessed his sin, he began to experience the blessedness and peace that come with guidance and forgiveness from God.

You do not have to continue to suffer. Get out of your own way _____ [insert your name]. Open up your heart and then your mouth to our loving, compassionate, and forgiving God--Get transparent. Get honest. Get forgiven. And once the weight lifts off your heart, your shoulders, and your spirit--Rejoice! Because you are free!

Psalm 33

This psalm is perfectly placed after Psalm 32. After we confess our sins and receive God's forgiveness, it is time to praise Him. Today's psalm begins with a call to worship the Lord through singing. When we confess our sins to God there is nothing separating our communion with Him; we have a static-free line. Our shame is gone. Our guilt is gone. Our fear is gone. Our doubt is gone.

We are implored to not only sing our praise to God, but to do so with others in the assembly. When God frees you from sin through the extension of forgiveness, can anyone tell? Does anyone know about it? Are you singing the same old songs, as if you were still burdened and bound by your sin or do you "sing to him a new song; play skillfully, and shout for joy"? (vs. 3) My pastor, Rev. Dr. Cynthia L. Hale likes to say that "if the love of God lives within you, your face ought to know about it." Likewise, your praise should be proportionate to the way that God has blessed you. If you would customarily sing "How Great Thou Art" let people hear you singing "Blessed Assurance." If the people in your carpool would normally hear "Nobody Greater" then put on "This is Day." If you'd usually sit still during worship, then stand to your feet, lift up holy hands, and dance before the Lord. If a change has come over you, which is exactly what we experience when we are forgiven, then let your praise show it.

In the blank space below, write a few song lyrics to your "new song." I hear you; you're not a songwriter. That is perfectly ok. You are not attempting to enter into a new career, but instead are simply praising God in your own words. No one can tell your story as well as you. What do you think, feel, and know about God delivering you from sin? What does it feel like to be blessed/happy as a result of God's extension of forgiveness?

Psalm 34

David continues his pattern of praise today. He begins with a firm commitment to praise God. This commitment to give God praise is not contingent on anything. It is not based on his feelings, the circumstances of his life, or the opinions of others. David "will extol the Lord at all times." (vs. 1) Next, David makes a very direct request for us to glorify God with him (vs. 3). While David's request to join him in praise and worship was indirect in the previous psalm, he threw caution to the wind in this psalm and directly asked us to join him in this psalm.

David knew that the hearer would question his commitment to praise God and therefore spends verses 4-7 explaining his reasoning. In making his case, David explained how he sought the Lord and then God answered and delivered him (vs. 4). After presenting his evidence, David made a profound closing statement in verse 8, "taste and see that the Lore is good." David believes in God and the Word so much that he calls us to try Him. We are called to feed on the Lord through His Word and everything God has for us. David drew near to God and found that the Lord is good!

Not only does David encourage us to try God for ourselves, he gives us a roadmap to guide us down the path of trusting God through obedience to His Word. He implores us to live righteously:

- **Listen to God (vs. 11)**
- **Desire what is good (vs. 12)**
- **Not speak evil or lies (vs. 13)**
- **Pursue what is right (vs. 14)**
- **Expect the best (vs. 15)**
- **Cry out to God (vs. 17)**

Which of these elements do you need to improve on? List them below and then lift them up to God in prayer.

_____

_____

_____

_____

Ask God to help you in the areas where you are weak and keep you in the areas of strength. "Ask and it will be given to you; seek and you will find; knock and the door will be opened to you" (Matthew 7:7). If you think that you are too far-gone in sin, transgressions, or fleshly existence to live righteously... Stop! Read this psalm again. David is not an exception to the rule; he is evidence of the faithfulness of God. What does the Word say? "The Lord redeems his servants; no one will be condemned who takes refuge in him" (vs. 22). Take refuge in Him... Taste and see!

Psalm 35

As I read this psalm, it seemed that I was reading another gripe session between David and God about his enemies. You too may have approached this text with impatience. I hope you overcame the urge to rush through the text. If not, read the psalm again. Did you see anything different this time? Hidden in the middle of this chapter seems to be a complaint about David's friends or loved ones, not about his enemies.

In verse 12, David lamented to the Lord that he received evil in return for the good deeds he committed. He fasted and prayed when "they" were sick in verse 13. He mourned and wept when they did not get better in verse 14. Although the Bible encourages us to love our neighbors as ourselves, if we got really honest, most people do not make this type of investment in their enemies. Although some of us are saved enough to avoid pursuit of our enemies or poor treatment of them, we are not fasting and praying on their behalf. Help us Lord! We ask God, is this what you want us to do? Do you really expect us to intercede for those who pursue us (vs. 3), who rejoice when we fall (vs. 15), and who mock us (vs. 16)? Absolutely! God commands you to "love your enemies and pray for those who persecute you" (Matthew 5:44).

This text was not about David's friends. Although it may sound like David was talking about the behavior of his friends, he was actually referring to lengths he went to for Saul. Saul has become notoriously known as an enemy of David. Saul tried to personally kill David and plotted to have the Philistines kill him in 1 Samuel 16. "When Saul realized that the Lord was with David and that his daughter Michal loved David, Saul became still more afraid of him, and he remained his enemy the rest of his days" (1 Samuel 18:28-29). Note that the text says, "all the rest of his days." Saul continued to pursue David and attempted to bring him to death until the day he died; but David prayed and fasted for Saul. Whoa!

Can you do that? Can you pray for your enemies? Can you petition God on their behalf? Luke 6:28 calls us to "bless those who curse you, pray for those who mistreat you." You must not only pray for your loved ones, your friends, and those in your corner, you must also petition heaven for our foes. I challenge you to spend the next three days praying for your enemies. Write the names of up to three enemies/foes/opposing forces below and pray for them. Don't call down the fire of God on their heads, but ask God to show you how to pray for them and then obediently and systematically pray for them. Lets see how God responds.

_____

_____

_____

_____

_____

_____

_____

Psalm 36

As I read this Psalm of David I found myself saying, "wow, our God is BIG!" On the surface this psalm was about his enemies, as were the majority of the preceding psalms, but on the other side of the familiar was something new. From verses 5-9, David expressed the vastness of God's emotions, actions, resources, and being. Our God is BIG and possesses abundant ability as well.

God's love reaches extremely far. David said that it reaches to the heavens (vs.5). How high are the heavens? We do not know, but they are higher than anything we can imagine or reach, right? God's love is like that, it can reach us wherever we are; "neither death, nor life, nor angels, nor principalities, nor powers, nor things present, nor things to come, nor height, nor depth, nor any other creature, shall be able to separate us from the love of God, which is in Christ Jesus our Lord" (Romans 8:38-39). Jesus brought us close to God through the sacrifice of His life; so close that we can never be separated from God's love.

God's faithfulness also has infinite reach, because it is a part of who He is...God IS faithful. He does not simply act faithfully, He IS faithful. What does it mean to say that God is faithful? One who is faithful is steadfast, trustworthy, and reliable. Our God is all of that and so much more. Our God is always there and will always be there for us. Deuteronomy 31:6 promises that God will never leave you or forsake you. Sounds pretty faithful to me. Can you think of a time that God did not come through? No, right? You may not have gotten what you wanted or received it when you wanted it, but God came through with exactly what you needed, when you needed it. Faithfulness. David goes on to talk about the righteousness, justice, and refuge of God, which are equally as vast and wonderful as the other characteristics of God.

David also brags about the resources of God, which are plentiful. In Psalm 24:1 we learned that "the earth is the Lord's, and everything in it, the world, and all who live in it," so how could His resources be anything other than abundant? God owns everything and therefore has everything at His disposal. In verse

8 of this psalm, David calls us to feast on the abundance of God's house and drink from God's river of delights. We have access to all the resources of God as His children. Not only does God possess all that you need and the ability to provide all you need, He wants to take care of you. "And my God will meet all your needs according to the riches of his glory in Christ Jesus" (Philippians 4:19). As one who is faithful, God will take care of you.

Yes, our God is BIG. He is able. God is willing. "Now to him who is able to do immeasurably more than all we ask or imagine, according to his power that is at work within us" (Ephesians 3:20). I implore you to trust in our BIG God today and every day! Whether you need to experience the vastness of His love, faithfulness, righteousness, justice, refuge, or resources today, trust that God has your back and will not disappoint you.

Psalm 37

Today's psalm reminded me of all the times that I felt frustrated about evildoers getting away with wrongdoing. I recalled small things like lie-telling, backbiting, making life difficult for others, or even blaming others for their actions. The big things crossed my mind like what happened today in Boston when innocent people were killed and injured as they crossed the finish line of the Boston Marathon as a bomb exploded. If you are anything like me, you've asked God, complained to God, and even gotten upset with God for allowing children to be abused, greedy people to embezzle funds, and drunk drivers to take the lives of other people. How long God? If you have ever felt this way, you are not alone.

David was tired of the wicked prevailing and the righteous remaining stagnant or failing. He wanted to know what was going on and he took his frustrations to God. The evil men around David plotted (vs. 12), schemed (vs. 7, 32), did not pay their debts (vs. 21), and used their power for personal gain (vs. 14). It would be one thing if all this wrongdoing got them nowhere, but they seemed to succeed in their ways (vs. 7). God was persistent in His response to all of the foolishness that concerned David—do not worry about it. God begins His reply by telling David "do not fret because of evil men" (vs. 1). Again, in verse 7 God says, "do not fret" and then again in verse 8, "do not fret." Although the actions of the evil were wearing David out and worrying him, God was not concerned in the least bit.

Why do we get all frazzled about things, when we are children of the Most High God? Why do we worry about things that don't even make God's radar? Because we are human. Fortunately, God is concerned with what concerns us; even if He has already worked the situation out in His sovereign plan. God simply asks that we "be still before the Lord and wait patiently for Him" (vs. 7). God has got this thing under control. "[His] eyes saw [your] unformed body; all the days ordained for [you] were written in [God's] book before one of them came to be" (Psalm 139:16). God is omniscient. He is all seeing and all knowing. "His understanding has no limit" (Psalm 147:5). We have to trust that He knows best and has planned for the best.

Bad things may be happening all around us, but we must trust that God knows. Remember, God works all things together for His good (Romans 8:28). While you think God is sleeping on the job, He has already planned a better response to your circumstance then you can ever think or ask. Look at what God told David about evildoers. They:

- **Won't be able to last (vs. 2)**
- **Will be brought to justice (vs. 6)**
- **Will be cut off (vs. 9)**
- **Will perish (vs. 10)**
- **Will bring harm back on themselves (vs. 15)**
- **Will lose power (vs. 17)**
- **Will vanish (vs. 20)**
- **Will be destroyed (vs. 38)**

But as for the righteous, God will help and deliver you (vs. 40). God only asks that you be patient (vs. 7), avoid sin (vs.27), and be obedient (vs. 34). Do not fret because evildoers seem to advance. There advancement is short-lived. Your reward is eternal.

Psalm 38

Today we meet David on the other side of sin. He had sinned and was rebuked by God. We were created to be in constant fellowship and communion with God and sin gets in the way of that relationship. Like static in the telephone, which blocks communication from one end of a telephone call to another, sin interrupts, blocks, and separates our connection with God. Sin separates us from Him (Isaiah 59:2) and therefore is antithetical to our raison d'être; hence the reason God hates sin. "The wages of sin is death" (Romans 6:23). Just as a flower begins to die the moment it is separated from its roots in the ground, we too die when we are separated from God. God is our source and our sustainer; we are lifeless without Him.

God hates sin so much that He must respond. Like a parent who disciplines their child when they do wrong, God rebukes us. Hebrews 12:6 teaches us that God's discipline is an act of love. Why do parents discipline or rebuke their children? To teach them; to deter them and to protect them. The same is true of God. This is the place that we met David. He was in the midst of being rebuked in the form of sickness. Like a child seeking to avoid time out, a spanking, or a scolding, David begs for mercy; "O Lord, do not rebuke me in your anger or discipline me in your wrath" (vs. 1). He could not handle God's discipline and asked God not to treat him as his sins deserved; "my guilt has overwhelmed me like a burden too heavy to bear" (vs. 4).

David spends 13 verses rehearsing all the reasons that he needs God to lighten the load of his punishment. His spirits are low (vs. 6), his body hurts (vs. 7-8), people have abandoned him (vs. 11-12), and he can't take anymore (vs. 17). It is all too much for David. I can imagine God listening to David and being unmoved by David's reasoning. Like a parent listening to all the reasons why they should choose a different punishment for their child, I can imagine God saying to Himself, "give me something good David." David finally turns the corner in verse 18 when he says "I confess my iniquity; I am troubled by my sin." Ok, David finally gets it and admits to doing wrong.

Do you own up to your wrongdoing? Or do you try to explain to God why you should not be punished? God calls us to be honest with ourselves and with Him when we sin. "If we confess our sins, he is faithful and just and will forgive us our sins and purify us from all unrighteousness" (1 John 1:9). God wants us to confess our sins, with a repentant heart (i.e. a genuine desire to omit that sin from our lives and not repeat it); God will do the rest. He will forgive us and clean us up. If we make excuses or focus solely on God's rebuke, we are not truly repentant. If we want God's mercy, we must be prepared to confess our sins.

Confess your sins to God. Get honest with yourself and God about your wrongdoing. Then watch the move of God in your life.

Psalm 39

Today, David is in a similar place as in the previous psalm; in the midst of discipline from God for his sinful behavior (vs.11). He does not know what to say or what to do. He is attempting to remain silent in the midst of his trial, so as not to give the wicked anything to use against him or God. As we have seen through our reading of the Book of Psalms, David had a lot of enemies and they did not cut him any slack. During this particular trial, the wicked were blaspheming God and criticizing David in the midst of his affliction. David was concerned that if he shared with us just how difficult this trial was and the grave impact that the Lord's rebuke was having on him that it would make God look bad.

Have you ever been concerned about making God look bad or about disappointing God? If so, you are not alone. Moses felt inadequate to lead the people of Israel out of Egypt (Exodus 3), Jeremiah was concerned about his qualifications to be a prophet (Jeremiah 1:6), and Jesus even asked God to keep him from going to the cross (Luke 22:42). Each of these pillars of the faith went to God for direction in the midst of these situations, just as David did in Psalm 39. David was not only honest about his feelings of inadequacy; he was also transparent about his ignorance as to how to proceed. He cried "but now, Lord, what do I look for? My hope is in you. Save me from all my transgressions; do not make me the scorn of fools" (vs. 7-8). David may not have known what to do, but he knew where to turn. He knew who would sustain him and who would bring him out — the Lord.

Can you commit to seeking the Lord, even when you are being disciplined for your sin? David's petition of the Lord reminds me of a child wanting to be held by their parent after receiving a spanking. The same person who rebuked you, is the same person that you want to comfort you. As children of God, we are just like that 5 year old being rocked to sleep after a spanking; we still need to be held. Run to God. Get honest. Trust Him to comfort you and bring you through.

Psalm 40

We seem to meet David on the other side of his cries for mercy and healing today. He begins this psalm testifying to the goodness of God and all that God had done for him. This writing provides a great framework for our best evangelical tool—our testimony. When we tell people where we've been, what God did, and how great God is, we are preaching a sermon that no one else can preach. No one can talk about YOUR God, like you. No one can tell YOUR story like you. The same rings true for David. He is sharing with others his testimony.

There is a shift in verse 6. David begins to analyze what he has been through. On the other side of his trial David seems to have some clarity that he did not have while going through the situation. We've all been there before. In the bottom of our pit, all we can see is the pit. We can't see any way out, nor can we think of what we should be doing in the pit. Hindsight is 20/20. David seems to realize that what he thought God wanted from him is worlds apart from what God was actually seeking during his trial. David says in verses 6-8:

Sacrifice and offering you did not desire —
but my ears you have opened —
burnt offerings and sin offerings you did not require.
Then I said, "Here I am, I have come —
it is written about me in the scroll.
I desire to do your will, my God;
your law is within my heart.

During Old Testament times, Israel offered sacrifices as atonement for their sins. The people brought various types of sacrifices to the tabernacle as an offering to God. These offerings were burned and offered to God in place of the blood of the sinner. Leviticus 17:11 teaches that "it is the blood that makes atonement for one's life." Since sin results in separation from God, these sacrifices were used to reconcile the sinner back to God. Instead of a bull, goat, or dove, God wanted something different from David this time; God did not want an animal substitute, he wanted David's obedience. God wanted David to live a "yes life"- a life totally surrendered to Him.

God wants the same from us. He wants us to do His will. "Your kingdom come, your will be done, on earth as it is in heaven" (Matthew 6:10). Can you say this and mean it? Can you live this today? This is what God wanted from David and it is what He wants from us. Not another animal on the altar, but a life of surrender and obedience. This is the best sacrifice that we could offer God today. Submit your will to God today.

Psalm 41

This psalm concludes a collection of four psalms. Each of these psalms was related to the illness David experienced due to his sin. David sought God's merciful healing in each of these psalms. Not only was David seeking healing, but he also wanted God to silence the taunts of his enemies. David's friends had even turned against him.

Have you ever been there? In a low place, for whatever reason, and instead of offering a helping hand people kicked you while you were down? Did they talk about you behind your back and in your face? Did they watch you suffer without showing compassion or sympathy? This is exactly where David was in these psalms. To make matters worse, David had brought his suffering on himself. Let us not forget that God was rebuking him for his sin.

As I read this collection of psalms, I couldn't help but feel sorry for David. Yes, he had sinned, but he was human. God's punishment seemed a bit harsh. "For all have sinned and fall short of the glory of God" (Romans 3:23). Sin was in David's DNA, just as it is in ours. As a descendant of Adam and Eve, David could not help his sinful nature and neither can we. At some point, each of us will sin and do sin. Most of us sin more than we are aware. But David recognized his sin and confessed it, so why does it seem that God punished him so severely and so long? Doesn't 1 John 1:9 say, "if we confess our sins, he is faithful and just and will forgive us our sins and purify us from all unrighteousness"? The Word of God is true and so were David's confessions, but pause for just one minute. There are some things that we do not know. We do not know the amount of time that passed between Psalms 38 and 41. These psalms could have been written all in one day, over a few days, or even a few weeks. Just because these Psalms are grouped together does not mean they only span four days. How long is God allowed to rebuke us? God is sovereign, right? We also do not know how many times David had committed this sin, confessed it, and God had forgiven him without rebuke. We cannot read into the text our assumptions about the factual situation.

Ultimately we have to trust that God knew what was best for David. God knew David before he was born. He saw his unformed body and ordained a plan for him in His book of life (Psalm 139:16). Whatever God had in store for David required this type of rebuke, deterrent, and response from God. We have to exercise this same kind of trust with respect to our own lives. "Many are the plans in a person's heart, but it is the Lord's purpose that prevails" (Proverbs 19:21). God has "got this" and He has you. Remember that God has "plans to prosper you and not to harm you, to give you a future and a hope" (Jeremiahs 29:11). If God sees fit to discipline you, even to the point of allowing you to suffer, trust that it will all work together for your good (Romans 8:28).

Psalm 42

This psalm is a Prayer of Korah (one of the leaders of the Levitical choir appointed by David to serve in the temple). This psalm is one of my favorites. Although the psalmist is praying for deliverance, which suggests that he was in the midst of crisis, I connect with his words. I can feel his anguish and sincerity. He begins with a cry, "as the deer pants for streams of water, so my soul pants for you, O God. My soul thirsts for God, for the living God" (vs. 1-2). He is desperate for God. Just as the deer depends on water, he recognizes his dependence on God. Have you ever been there? Thirsty for God? My pastor likes to say "there is a God shaped hole in each of us that only God can fill." Not only do I believe that, but I also experience that frequently. I used to think unbelievers who had not responded to the call of Christ only experienced this hole. I have come to experience this void as a result of my sin, in the midst of tests/trials, when I have gone too long without worshipping, and even when God is stretching me. All of those situations make me thirsty for God. I need to be in His presence so that the hole within me can be refilled.

When was the last time you thirsted for God? What did you do about it? Write your answer below:

_____

_____

_____

_____

_____

Korah was not only experiencing separation from God, but was also absent from the temple. He was out of fellowship with other believers and longed to reconnect. In verse 4, he is quite reflective. "These things I remember as I pour out my soul: how I used to go with the multitude, leading the procession to the house of God, with shouts of joy and thanksgiving among the festive throng." Our call to follow Christ is not an invitation to live inside a bubble where it is only God and us. This call is an invitation into a body — the Body of Christ, where we are but one part of the Body. Let me be clear, it is impossible to follow Christ in the way God intends without being connected to the Body of Christ (i.e. a member of the church universal and local). Hebrews 10:25 implores us not to "forsake the assembly," because our connection is vital to the viability of the church and to our spiritual development. When we separate from the Body we are not only disconnected from other believers, we are disconnected from Christ. "Now you are the body of Christ, and each one of you is a part of it" (1 Corinthians 12:27). Korah felt this separation and desperately wanted to reconnect.

Are you separated from God? It is time to reconnect. Are you separated from the Body? It is time to reconnect. That thirst your feel can only been quenched by God. "Put your hope in God" (vs. 11). Allow Him to fill that hole inside of you.

Psalm 43

Today, Korah is praying for deliverance from the hands of the enemy. He desperately wants to be restored to God's presence. As I read this psalm it sounds like the writer has thrown his hands up in surrender, asking God to have His way. "Vindicate me," he says to God. Defend me. Korah calls on God to serve as his lawyer "plead my cause against an ungodly nation; rescue me from deceitful and wicked men" (vs. 1). Have you ever found yourself in a situation that you knew you could not talk yourself out of? Did you know you weren't savvy enough, smart enough, or influential enough to wiggle out of whatever circumstance you found yourself in? How did you handle it? Did you try to get yourself out of it anyway or did you call the Lawyer of all lawyers to handle your defense?

When Korah asked God to vindicate him, he placed his concern and his situation in God's hands. This was an act of trust. Although it may appear nonsensical, your situation is safer in God's hands than your own. Scripture calls you to "trust in the Lord with all your heart and lean not on your own understanding" (Proverbs 3:5). Why? Why would God tell you to let go of things as important as being concerned about your job, family, finances, health, home, etc.? The reason that you want to hold on is the very reason you are called to let go; these matters are vitally important to you.

When we let go, we are letting God grab hold of the situation. What safer place is there than inside the hands of God? What better place for your situation or concern than on God's to-do list? Matthew 6:8 teaches us that "your Father knows what you need before you ask him." God knows best. Although you are on earth, in the midst of your circumstance, you do not know the future. You do not have a complete view of the plan for you life. You will not have full revelation until you meet Jesus face to face; "For now we see only a reflection as in a mirror; then we shall see face to face. Now I know in part; then I shall know fully, even as I am fully known" (1 Corinthians 13:12).

If you can follow the lead of Korah and place your situation completely into the hands of God, you will have nothing to worry about. "Do not worry about tomorrow, for tomorrow will worry about itself. Each day has enough trouble of its own" (Matthew 6:34). God has it all under control. Once you let go, you will find yourself in a place of peace. This is the ultimate reason that God wants to handle our concerns, because He wants us to live lives of peace. Korah was released from his worries when he decided to trust in God. "Why are you downcast, O my soul? Why so disturbed within me? Put your hope in God, for I will yet praise him, my Savior and my God" (vs. 5). Korah essentially said to himself, "get yourself together; there is nothing left to worry about because God has it!" Decide to trust God today.

Psalm 44

Once again, the people of Israel are the objects of scorn among the nations. People are looking at them, pointing, and mocking. Gossip is flying and their credibility is being questioned. To make matters worse, they are being defeated in battled (vs. 9-12) and shamed before their enemies (vs.13-16). Israel had grown used to being on top; they had grown accustomed to being victorious. Now that they weren't winning, they did not know how to take it. They were at a loss. Besides, didn't God promise in Deuteronomy 28:13 to "make you the head, not the tail. If you pay attention to the commands of the Lord your God that I give you this day and carefully follow them, you will always be at the top, never at the bottom." Something was really out of whack.

The main reason that Korah was at a loss was because Israel had done nothing wrong. The promise of victory in Deuteronomy 28:13 was contingent on Israel's obedience to God's commands. According to Psalm 44, Israel had been faithful to God's promises. The writer proclaims in verse 20 that the people had kept God's commandments in Exodus 20:3-4; they had placed no other gods before the Lord and worshipped God alone. Korah was confused by their losing state. They had gone out to battle and "faced death all day long" for God's sake, so why were they suffering defeat and embarrassment?

Have you ever found yourself in a similar position? You did what you were "supposed" to do. You followed God's commandment or the promptings of the Holy Spirit. You stepped out on faith and refused to allow fear to be your guide. But instead of a rich reward, you seemed to suffer a devastating defeat. Is that you? Have you been there? As you can see, you are not alone. You are in good company. There is much witness to this very situation. Why do you think Jesus said "a prophet is not without honor except in his own town, among his relatives and in his own home"? (Mark 6:4) Or Stephen was stoned in Act 7:59? Or how do you think Moses felt in Exodus 15:24 when the people grumbled against him after He led them out of slavery? Disappointment is a part of life and so is the hard and often harsh reality that sometimes things do not work out how we would like or expect.

As I read this text, I saw God's sovereignty all over it. God is in control. He is in charge. Yahweh is the decider. Sometimes the reason that things play out the way they do is not apparent to us. "As the heavens are higher than the earth, so are my ways higher than your ways and my thoughts than your thoughts" (Isaiah 55:9). Accept the fact that sometimes you will not know or even understand life, circumstances, and the ways of God. The sooner we accept God's sovereignty, the sooner we will save ourselves from unnecessary stress, grief, and disappointment.

Take a moment and say these four words out loud, "God is in control." Say them again, and again, and again. Say them until they get deep down in your spirit. It will change your entire day.

Psalm 45

Today's psalm is a Love Song written to commemorate a wedding. The songwriter writes about the marriage of a king to his bride; a throne, scepter, and majesty are mentioned throughout the psalm. Each line is filled with excitement, joy, and anticipation. Unlike many of the other psalms that we have read, this psalm is airy, light, and carefree. This is a joyous occasion. Some have identified Solomon, the son of David, as the king referenced in this psalm. However, this psalm seems to point to one greater than King Solomon--Jesus Christ, the King of kings. Although Solomon was a respected king of Israel and worthy of human honor, the chief musician would not sing about him during worship in the sanctuary. This would be blasphemy. This psalm is about Jesus Christ and His bride, the church. The church is referred to as the bride of Christ throughout scripture (Ephesians 5:23, Revelation 19:6-21; 22:17)

The writer rejoices over the various dimensions of Christ. He begins by setting Jesus apart from every other man who has ever walked the earth; "you are the most excellent of men" (vs. 2). Israel was blessed with a number of great leaders, Moses, Deborah, Samuel, David, and Solomon were among them, but Jesus surpassed them all. Korah goes on to say "your lips have been anointed with grace, since God has blessed you forever" (vs. 2). Jesus was sinless and spotless (1 Peter 1:19), gentle (Matthew 11:29), and compassionate (John 8:1-11). He was like none other.

Korah writes about Jesus as victorious warrior in verses 3-5. Jesus is not only a meek and mild servant, but He is a warrior. God has been at war with Satan and sin since Adam and Eve chose autonomy in Genesis 3 and enmity was placed between humanity and the serpent. Jesus died on the cross to save humanity and to defeat Satan (Colossians 2:13-15). He will return as the Lion of Judah and defeat all his enemies (Revelation 19:11).

Jesus is also a righteous king. Just as Jesus was human, He was also divine. After Jesus rose from the grave, as reflected in Mark 16, He ascended to heaven in Luke 24:51. Jesus Christ is reigning now in heaven, seated at the right hand of the Father (Colossians 3:1). Korah gives Him praise for being a just and righteous king in verses 6 and 7. If the people of Israel recognized the need to honor their earthly kings, how much more worthy was the King of kings and the Lord of lords of their continuous praise?

The remainder of the psalm is spent describing the royal wedding between Christ and His Church. Preparation of the bride is addressed in verses 10-13. Do you believe the Church is ready to be joined with Christ? Today, the Church is filled with internal conflict and has a poor external reputation, but this will not always be the case; one day it shall be a glorious bride, spotless, blameless, and without spot or wrinkle (Ephesians 5:27). In order to prepare for her Bridegroom the Church must lay down its worldly ways and connections and become a true reflection of God.

As a member of Christ's Church, what things do you need to forget/let go of to help prepare God's Church to be joined with Christ?

Psalm 46

Today, the writer expresses firm confidence in the Lord. You can hear the certainty of the writer as he makes each claim about the Lord. There is no hint of insecurity or doubt; Korah is 100% convinced about God's ability take care of His people. What about you? Do you know that God will handle everything concerning you today?

Korah boasts, "God is our refuge and strength, an ever-present help in trouble" (vs. 1). Do you wonder how this writer can be so sure? Look at verses 8-10, he has measurable proof. The writer challenges the hearer of this song to "come and see what the Lord has done" and then goes on to list some examples. "The desolations he has brought on the earth. He makes wars cease to the ends of the earth. He breaks the bow and shatters the spear; he burns the shields with fire" (v. 9). The writer is confident because he has seen what God has done before and has no reason to believe that God will not move on behalf of His people again. What has God done in your life? Has He ever delivered you from evil? Healed your body? Protected you from danger? Provided for your financial needs? Comforted you when heartbroken? I challenge you to trust God to do it again. God has done all of that for me and He will do it for you. I am not a special case. God will not do for me, what He is unwilling to also do for you or any of His children. God does not show favoritism (Acts 10:34).

The writer is also confident because God has spoken directly to him concerning his situation. Look at verse 10; "He says, 'Be still, and know that I am God; I will be exalted among the nations, I will be exalted in the earth.'" Note the words "he says." God has spoken. When God speaks, there is nothing left to say, do, or worry about. God had spoken to Korah and therefore he is confident. God said, "I've got this." What has God spoken to you about your situation? Have you asked Him? God is in the prayer answering business. He promises to answer, if we ask. ""Ask, and it will be given to you, seek and you will find; knock, and it will be opened to you" (Matthew 7:7), If you want to know something about your life, your circumstances, or your future, ask God.

Once God speaks, rest comfortably knowing that God's got you. That is exactly what Korah did. He asked God and received an answer. He reflected back on God's reputation and trusted Him to remain consistent with His past. Then he walked in the assurance that "the Lord Almighty is with us; the God of Jacob is our fortress" (vs. 11). Can you do that today? Give it a try.

Psalm 47

Today, I read this psalm exactly seven days after the bombing at the Boston Marathon. The United States of America is in a season of mourning and turmoil once again. Its citizens sit in a seat that has become far too familiar. We were here during the bombing in Atlanta during the Olympic Games and also after the Oklahoma City bombing. We were here during the attacks on the World Trade Center and during the mass shootings in Columbine, New Town, and Aurora. People are hurting, confused, angry and devastated—all at the same time. These waves of emotion are being expressed on the world's stage; the nations know that America is going through.

In the midst of this struggle, God is still God. Lets peak ahead at Psalm 145:3. It says that "Great is the Lord and most worthy of praise; His greatness no one can fathom." Notice that this proclamation does not contain any contingencies or "if/then" statements. It is not qualified in any way; God is great, period. It does not state that if all is well in our nation, our families, or personal lives that God is great, but instead a definitive, unchanging, unquestionable fact is stated-God is great. Since God is great, He is worthy of praise. Praise is not based on how we feel or the circumstances surrounding us. Praise is due God because He is God. Our praise is not about us at all, it is all about God. Yes, we, as the human beings created to worship and serve Him are called to offer praise to God, but God will receive His praise, even if the rocks have to cry out (Luke 19:40).

Can you praise God in the midst of crisis? Lets try. Lets apply the "Psalm 43" formula together.

Verse 1 tells us to clap our hands and to shout to God with joy. What has God EVER done for you that is worthy of a standing ovation? What move of God is worthy of you yelling "thank you"? Perhaps God has healed your body or protected you in a car accident. Speak five reasons that you have to be thankful, while saying thank you in between each reason. Clap while you doing so (e.g. thank you God...clap, clap, for saving me, clap, clap). If you need a little inspiration, look at verses 2-5 to see what Korah had to clap and sing about.

Verse 6 tells us to sing our praises to God. Turn on your favorite praise song or pull out your hymnal. Turn it up, way up. Now sing like your life depends on it. God loves to hear you sing praise to Him, no matter what it sounds like. ☺

Clapping, shouting, singing and even dancing before the Lord serves many purposes. It lifts up the name of the Lord. It encourages your heart as you are reminded of the greatness of God. It witnesses to others about what you believe and in whom you trust. It also irritates, aggravates, and then defeats the enemy. Read 2 Chronicles 20. This passage tells the story of how King Jehoshaphat and his army defeated the people of Moab and Ammon with their praise. You too confuse and defeat the enemy every time you choose to praise God in spite of it all!

Psalm 48

In this Psalm of Korah, the writer celebrates the security found in the City of God (vs. 1). Kings are filled with terror and pain and then retreat when they encounter the City of God (vs. 4-6). Its enemies are destroyed (vs. 7). It was not the City's army, citadels, walls, or weapons that kept it secure, but God's presence. It was God that kept the City and its people safe and terrified its enemies (vs. 3).

Security is defined as the state of being free from danger. Who do you look to keep you safe? Your parents? Your significant other? The police, army, or firefighters? The government? Ultimately, God is the source of your protection; "the Lord is faithful. He will establish you and guard you against the evil one" (2 Thessalonians 3:3). Often we are disappointed when other people cannot be to us what only God can be. When you feel unsafe, unprotected, or insecure today, pray the words of 2 Samuel 22:3-4:

"My God, my rock, in whom I take refuge, my shield, and the horn of my salvation, my stronghold and my refuge, my savior; you save me from violence. I call upon the Lord, who is worthy to be praised, and I am saved from my enemies."

The writer had proof of God's faithfulness. He said, "as we have heard, so have we seen in the city of the Lord Almighty, in the city of our God: God makes her secure forever" (vs. 8). He had heard the testimonies of others and was encouraged by them. Have you ever sat in amazement and listened to another person talk about who God had been to them and how He blessed them? What did it do for you? The Bible tells us that "faith comes from hearing the message, and the message is heard through the word about Christ" (Romans 10:17). Listening to people testify to Jesus builds our faith.

Korah also saw God move for himself. What has God shown you? Sometimes we get so bogged down by our current crisis or trials that we forget to look for God's footprints. When God shows up in our lives He leaves footprints. Each time He heals your body a footprint is left behind. When He provides for your needs, He leaves a footprint. Whenever unity is brought in your family, a footprint is all over that transformation. Korah felt secure in his present circumstance because he trusted in the footprints that were laid all over his life and the City of God. Look for the footprints in your life. God provides to "never leave you nor forsake you" in Deuteronomy 31:6. If He has protected you before, He'll do it again!

Psalm 49

In this psalm, we read a word of wisdom about persons who foolishly rely on their wealth and personal strength instead of God. Unlike the wise persons mentioned in Psalm 48 who found safety and protection in God, these people find security in the money in the bank, the cars they drive, the houses they live in, and their other worldly possessions. Korah has observed the attitudes of many rich persons and encourages those who are in awe by their wealth not to be disillusioned.

The writer first cautions all listeners against the stupidity of reliance upon wealth. He tells us that wealth will not bring protection on the day of evil. Ultimately, what can money do for you? Money will not allow us to "redeem the life of another" (vs. 7). Life is priceless. No amount of money will pay to save the life of a loved one. Can you put a limit on the amount of money you would be wiling to pay if your son, daughter, spouse, or friend was kidnapped? Would you tell the kidnapper to keep them if they asked you for $100,000? What about $500,000? One million, would be your cut off, right? Even if you did not have the demanded amount of funds, you would not say "my loved one is not worth that much money." Why? Because they are priceless to you, right? You can't quantify how much value they have in your life by a dollar figure.

How much more valuable is eternal life? Can you put a price tag on redeeming humanity back to God? There was a price—a life. Jesus Christ gave His life for us to be redeemed (John 3:16; Titus 2:14). Jesus did not give God money; "the ransom for a life is costly, no payment is ever enough" (vs. 8). Would you give your life for anything? For anyone one?

It is also not prudent to get bent out of shape by the wealth of the rich because their money cannot keep them from death (vs. 10). Everyone dies. Money may be able to buy you good medical treatment, but it cannot buy infinite life. We have all seen very wealthy people die from cancer, heart attacks, lupus, and other diseases. It did not matter how much money they had, their bodies still gave out and they passed from this life to the next.

Korah encourages us not to get caught up focusing on the rich man because "he is like the beasts that perish" (vs. 12).

It is easy to imagine that being rich would fix all our problems, especially in this financial climate. But it will not; this stream of thinking is faulty. Korah implores us to seek understanding instead of riches (vs. 20). Wise people know that we must "seek first his kingdom and his righteousness, and all these things will be given to you as well" (Matthew 6:33). It is in God and through God that we have everything we need. Don't believe the hype!

Psalm 50

In this Psalm of Asaph, the Lord calls His people, Israel, to account. Like the Korahites, the Asaphites were one of the families/guilds of musicians in the Jerusalem temple during the reign of King David. In contemporary terms, Asaph was a worship leader. This psalm was likely composed for a temple liturgy and therefore used for communal worship. The people of Israel were lead through this three-part psalm to reaffirm their commitment to God. First, was the announcement that God was calling His people to account (vs. 1-6). Second, came words of correction for the good intentioned person (vs. 7-15). Finally, came a harsh rebuke of the wicked (vs. 16-23).

God's first rebuke of Israel was about their sacrifices. Israel thought that God was dependent on their sacrifices, just as the pagan gods were dependent on those of its followers. God made it clear in this psalm that He is not a pagan god and does not operate like one. In verses 9-11, God tells Israel that He knows and owns all the animals on the planet and therefore does not need them from Israel. Why do we think that God needs us to fulfill His plans? We act as if God is sitting in heaven hoping and praying that we will conform to His will so that the world will go on. "The God who made the world and everything in it, being Lord of heaven and earth, does not live in temples made by man, nor is he served by human hands, as though he needed anything, since he himself gives to all mankind life and breath and everything" (Acts 17:24-25).

What can we possibly offer God? What can we give to Him that He does not already possess? We should serve God today because we need God and what He has to offer us; this was the message that God gave to Israel in Psalm 50. He tells them to "fulfill your vows to the Most High, and call on me in the day of trouble; I will deliver you, and you will honor me" (vs. 14-15). Israel had entered into a covenant with God to be their people and to have Him be their God (Exodus 6:7). This was a vow to honor God through their obedience, praise, and submission. As Christians, we made the same vow to submit to the lordship of Jesus Christ when we made our confession of faith (Romans 10:9-10).

God promises Israel that if they fulfill their vows, call upon Him, and honor Him, He will deliver them in their times of trouble. Are you submitted to the lordship of Jesus Christ? Are you offering the sacrifice of your life through obedience to the Word and keeping your vows?

Pray with me: *Lord, help me to honor you with my life today. I recognize that I need you to survive and I submit to your lordship.*

Psalm 51

If the psalms were written in the order they were placed and all were authored by the same person I would say that Israel learned the lesson that God was trying to teach them by the time they arrived at Psalm 51; that God does not need their sacrifices and that He is God regardless of what they do. At several points during this psalm, David expressly acknowledges that God is not impressed by animal sacrifice and finds it an inadequate response to David's sins. God wanted something more from David and He wants more from us. God wants our lives. "The sacrifices of God are a broken spirit; a broken and contrite heart O God, you will not despise" (vs. 17). What pleases God more than animal sacrifice is a humble heart; one willing to seek Him for mercy and forgiveness.

What is your response to sin? Are you effected? Do you feel remorseful? Do you repent? David did, after Nathan exposed his adultery with Bathsheba and his murder of Bathsheba's husband Uriah (2 Samuel 11-12). Psalm 51 reflects David's plea for mercy and forgiveness after being convicted. Although David's sin impacted Uriah, Bathsheba, and the people of Israel, their forgiveness was not most significant—God's forgiveness was key. David said, "against you, you only have I sinned and done what is evil in your sight" (vs. 4). He had violated God's law. He had murdered, committed adultery, and coveted his neighbor's household (Exodus 20:13-14, 17).

God has given each of us commandments through His Word; to disobey them is a sin against God (no matter who else is involved). When we are disobedient, we fail to demonstrate our love for God. How? John 14:15 says that if we love God we will keep his commandments. Our obedience is a demonstration of our love. David messed up and begged for forgiveness, he did not want God to wrongly believe that he did not love Him. The breach in their relationship was more than David could take. He was afraid of being cast out of God's presence and having the Holy Spirit taken from him, as he had already seen God do with Saul (vs. 11).

What is your prayer when you sin? David provides us with a good model for how to pray in response to our sin in this psalm. First, he acknowledged his sin as an offense against God. He admitted his wrong (vs. 3-5). Second, he asked God to clean him up. David did not want to commit the same sins (vs. 7-10). Third, he attempted to mend the breach in the relationship by acknowledging the repercussions of his wrongdoing (vs. 11-12) Fourth, David promised to glorify God through his wrongdoing by helping someone else (vs. 15-14). Finally, he promised to give God praise if he was shown mercy (vs. 15).

Give David's model a try today. David may have messed up big, but he also fessed up big. And as we know, God forgave him. Why? Because "if we confess our sins, he is faithful and just and will forgive us our sins and purify us from all unrighteousness" (1 John 1:9). God is just amazing like that. ☺

Psalm 52

David's message for us today: when your enemies are after you, sick God on them. As we have seen through our study, David had a lot of haters. Despite their attacks, he expressed fearless confidence in God and in God's ability to protect him.

It seems that we enter this text in the middle of a confrontation between David and one of his enemies. We do not know whether he was actually arguing with the individual, but that is the perspective from which this text seems to be written. David begins by asking his enemy why he was so boastful about his wrongdoing? (vs. 1) David is offended that this individual would do evil and brag about it. I can't say that I blame David. Have you ever had someone perform a wrongful act towards you and find out that they are telling everyone about what they did? Whether it was on the job, at school, or at church. It made you crazy, right? David's enemy was open and notorious about his evildoing. The nerve! Apparently David's enemy was not only boastful, but a gossiper, a deceiver, a liar, and a lover of evil (vs. 2-4). This man was a repeat offender that enjoyed wrongdoing and hurting others. We can usually handle those people who cross us once, but repeat offenders are simply unbearable. David's enemy possessed a flawed morality. He did not care about right versus wrong.

David had enough. He turned his enemy over to God. David had learned over the course of his life that sin was committed first and foremost against God, so his enemies conduct was not only offensive to him, but also to God. David also knew that as one of God's anointed that he was protected and that God did not take kindly to his enemy's vicious attacks (1 Chronicles 16:22). So David declared his enemy's ruin in verse 5-7 – God will slay you for what you have done! His enemy was going down. He told him that God would snatch him up, pluck him out his tent, and kill him – all as a result of his evildoing and attack of David. Our God does not play! So when your enemies come after you, remember that God has your back. You have nothing to fear or worry about, because God is concerned about you and will go after those who attempt to harm you. David not only believed it, he professed it, and so can you.

"Be strong and courageous. Do not be afraid or terrified because of them, for the Lord your God goes with you; he will never leave you nor forsake you" (Deuteronomy 31:6).

Psalm 53

Although this psalm was written thousands of years ago, it sounds like something we could write today. "The fool says in his heart, there is no God" (vs. 1). How many people, organizations, and groups could we say this about? Either because they actually profess that God does not exist or because they act like it. We could say that the Boston Marathon bombers acted as if there is no God and so did the killer in the Lone Star College shooting. The same could also be said about the members of Congress who act without regard to the needs of God's people or even about parents who abuse their children every day. David said, "they are corrupt, and their ways are vile" (vs. 1). Just as you can feel the sense of hopeless running rampant in our country today, as children die from street violence daily, you can also feel the hopelessness in Psalm 53. He cried out "there is no one who does good" (vs. 1). Is that how you feel? Like all hope is lost?

Although it is tempting to believe that God does not see all the destruction in the world, all the hatred in our country, and all the violence in our neighborhoods, resist the urge of hopelessness. We serve an all seeing, all knowing God. He sees you, He sees me, He sees us all. As David indicated in verse 2, "God looks down from heaven on the sons of men." God watches over His creation. We have nothing to fear because God is not only watching us, but He is with us.

We learn in this psalm that evil people will face their day. Even though the harm is done and it may seem like people got away with their crimes, transgressions, and sins they have not. David prophetically speaks about their future as if their destruction has already occurred. He says "then they were, overwhelmed with dread, where there was nothing to dread. God scattered the bones of those who attacked you; you put them to shame for God despised them" (vs. 5). God will devastate the ungodly that attack His people. Let's be clear. Although people may be foolish enough to think there is no God or act like God does not exist — He does exist and He will vindicate His people. God's curse will fall upon the evil and they will be defeated. Although we have no appreciation for the gravity of David's words in verse 5b, hopefully we can appreciate the sentiment. He describes the scattered corpses of a defeated army after God's great victory. It was a disgrace for a body to remain unburied in the ancient Near East, even an executed criminal was supposed to have a decent burial. Those who believe and act as if God does not exist face a fate lower than an executed criminal.

Do not be deceived: God cannot be mocked. A man reaps what he sows (Galatians 6:7). God's purposes and plans will not be thwarted by evil. "Oh, that salvation for Israel would come out of Zion! When God restores the fortunes of his people, let Jacob rejoice and Israel be glad!" (vs. 6) God is on mission to redeem all of creation. His plan will not be side stepped or sidetracked because people act foolishly, crazy, evil, or ungodly. People can claim not to believe in God if they choose, but "it is written: 'As surely as I live,' says the Lord, 'every knee will bow before me; every tongue will acknowledge God'" (Romans 14:11).

Psalm 54

Today, David prays desperately for God to save him from his enemies. Although the issue is a persistent one, there is something different about the prayer in Psalm 54. It is short, sweet, and to the point. He wants God to save him quickly.

Although long, persistent, and tarrying prayers serve their purpose, they are not always possible or practical. Sometimes, we have to get to God and urgently present our requests. I can imagine David running through the mountains with Saul's men in hot pursuit as he yelled out to God, "save me, O God, by your name; vindicate me by your might" (vs. 1). I am sure that the A.C.T.S. format of prayer (adoration, confession, thanksgiving and supplication) was the last thing on his mind as he dodged arrows aimed at his head. He got straight to the point—Save me!!!

Prayer is our method of communicating with God. Although we talk to God as we give Him praise and worship, we often are using the words of another, whether it is hymns, praise chorus, or the psalms. Prayer allows us to tell God exactly what is going on in our lives, in our own words. After David cried out to God, he plainly told God what was happening. "Strangers are attacking me; ruthless men seek my life—men without regard for God" (vs. 3). As God's friends, we are in intimate relationship with Him (John 15:15). How do you talk to your friends? Do you beat around the bush? Or use flowery language to tell a story? Is there a lot of pomp and circumstances when you talk? No, you come to them transparently, plainly, and honestly. God desires the same from us.

Next, David expressed confidence in God and His desire to respond to his request. "Surely God is my help; the Lord is the one who sustains me" (vs. 4). He knew that God had his back and would bring him out of his situation. David was also sure that he would be fine until God delivered him from the hand of Saul—his enemy. How confident are you in God? His ability? Do you really believe that "God will meet all your needs according to the riches of his glory in Christ Jesus"? (Philippians 4:19) If so, profess it. Live it.

It is easy to brag about God and His character during good times. It is when the rubber meets the road and times get hard that we really demonstrate what we believe. David trusted God to be a sustainer and He proved that in his darkest hour by calling out to God and expressing confidence that He would keep him until God brought him out of his trial. What do you believe today?

Psalm 55

David seeks the Lord because, once again, he is under attack. This would seem to be familiar territory for him. Besides David is always under attack, his enemies constantly pursue him, and he regularly needs vindication. But this time is different; it is not his enemies who are after him, it is a former friend. As if dealing with conflict is not hard enough, it is exasperated by the feelings of betrayal that we feel when the circumstance is with a friend. Instead of simply experiencing feelings of fear and anger, David is also distraught (vs. 2), and in anguish (vs. 4). David is hurt.

Have you ever been betrayed by a friend? Write a few words describing the situation and the emotions you felt below:

_____

_____

_____

_____

_____

_____

How did you handle the situation? Let's look at how David handled his encounter.

1. **He sought the Lord about it.** "Listen to my prayer, O God" (vs. 1). Far too often we take our situations to other individuals and not God. Although David is known for seeking wise counsel through Nathan, this psalm does not mention discussions with others.
2. **David was honest with himself and God about what he was feeling.** David was hurt and confused. He told God. We must get real with ourselves about our emotions and then real with God. It is only when we are honest, that we open ourselves up to be helped.
3. **He made his petition to God.** "Confuse the wicked, O Lord, confound their speech" (vs. 9). David wants the attacks of his frien-emy to stop. Although God knows our heart, He wants to hear from us about what we need.

4. **David leaves his request with God.** "Cast your cares on the Lord and he will sustain you" (vs. 22). We often take our petitions to God and then we take them back. Instead of allowing God to bring resolution to our situations, we try to resolve them ourselves. David left his prayer in God's hands to resolve.

5. **He expressed trust in God's ability to handle his concern.** "But as for me, I trust in you" (vs. 23). There is no point in taking a situation to God if we don't trust Him to handle it.

After reading Psalm 55, how will you handle your frien-emies differently in the future?

Psalm 56

Today, we meet David crying out to God, once again, for mercy while under attack. This time his life is threatened. When things occur in our lives, they seem really bad, until we experience something worse. That broken arm seems like nothing when you are diagnosed with cancer. That last break-up seems easy compared to the current one. That last boss appears "not so bad" compared to this tyrant. One trial puts the other in perspective. We have read about various attacks that David experienced from both friends and foes. Most of them involved slander, shunning, and abandonment, however this attack was on his life. The Philistines, the persistent enemies of Israel, had seized David in Gath.

Although David was afraid, he did what he had always done — expressed confident trust in God to deliver him (vs. 3). He did not trust himself or his army to deliver him, David trusted God. No matter how bad it seems we must not forsake our faith. "We live by faith, not by sight" (2 Corinthians 5:7). Can you commit to trust God when it gets really bad? It is easy to say that God is a provider, until we experience real lack in our lives or that He is a healer until we are sick. Trusting God to be what you need, when in need, is true faith.

There is a nugget in this psalm that I do not want us to overlook. After David laments to God about the things his enemies are doing he says, "What can mortal man do to me?" (vs. 4) With all David is experiencing — slander, seizure, and possibly death, he recognizes that the Philistines are not ultimately in control. At the point of his greatest fear, David remembers that God is on his side. "If God is for us, who can be against us?" (Romans 8:31) Although the book of Romans had yet to be written, David had the promises of God to lean on-- "Be strong and courageous. Do not be afraid or terrified because of them, for the Lord your God goes with you; he will never leave you nor forsake you" (Joshua 1:9). Since God had promised and kept His promise to Israel to be with them wherever they went, David knew that God would protect him even in the hands of the Philistines. What could they do to him?

Remember God's promise to never leave you or forsake you. If God is with you then "no weapon forged against you will prevail, and you will refute every tongue that accuses you" (Isaiah 54:17). If God has got you covered then you can boldly profess with David—what can mortal man do to me?! You are covered!

Psalm 57

Yesterday we talked about the promise God made in Deuteronomy 31:6 to never leave you or forsake you. Today, we learn a bit about how God keeps that promise. Have you ever wondered how the God of the entire universe is able to always make sure that you are cared and provided for? David gives us a bit of insight in verse 3; "He sends from heaven and saves me, rebuking those who hotly pursue me—God sends forth his love and his faithfulness."

God is always on duty. "For he looks to the ends of the earth and sees everything under the heavens" (Job 28:24). There is never a time that you are outside of God's sight. Most of the time that is good news. ☺ If we are honest, there are some things that we do not want God to see. You know, that anger, meanness, sharp tongue, fornication, adultery, or lying. While it may be true that those actions are embarrassing to us, when we think about God knowing about them, it is best for God to see them. In this psalm, David told us that God sends exactly what we need down from heaven and saves us. If God does not see our sin, He can't forgive us for it. If God does not see us in trouble, as He did David when he was running from Saul, He cannot deliver us.

My mother used to tell me that it was best for me to operate from a place of full disclosure with her. Her rationale was that she could not help me with what she did not know. Even when I had done wrong, was disobedient, or started the incident with another, it was always wise and prudent for her to know what REALLY happened so that she could help me and advocate for me. The same rings true for God. When we cry out to Him, He will respond. God will send His love and faithfulness because we are His children (vs. 3).

God may not always give us what we want, but He promises to give us exactly what we need. "Which of you, if your son asks for bread, will give him a stone? Or if he asks for a fish, will give him a snake? If you, then, though you are evil, know how to give good gifts to your children, how much more will your Father in heaven give good gifts to those who ask him!" (Matthew 7:9-11) When we are in need, God will send us what we need. Look for

God's answer to your prayers today. It may come through peace of mind or provision for a need. It may come through human support, comfort, or compassion. God may even send one of His angels to see about you. "Whatever you ask in my name, this I will do, that the Father may be glorified in the Son. If you ask me anything in my name, I will do it" (John 14:13-14).

Remember: God sends from the heavens!

Psalm 58

Today, David cries out to God about the then-current state of human affairs. He begs God to judge the rulers who corrupt justice. David desires for God to "take up" the cause of the righteous and advocate for their interests and needs. Although this psalm was written thousands of years ago, it feels like the writer could be speaking about today. This psalm is timeless.

On April 3, 2013, the Washington Post reported survey results that 91% of Americans desire expanded background checks on gun purchases. Then on April 17, 2013, the United States Senate voted to defeat a bill that would that would give the American people what they desire—better gun control. This vote came only four months after 20 children were shot to death in a school in Newton, Connecticut, two years after a member of Congress was shot in the head during a public shooting in Arizona, and after a bloody Easter weekend in Chicago where 25 people were wounded or killed by gun violence. Fifty-six people voted against the bill and 46 were in favor of it. Some of the opposition admitted that they voted against the bill because they did not want to be viewed as "helping the President," who is in favor of gun control.

David's cry for justice is echoed in 2013. The words of verse 2, "in your heart you devises injustice, and your hands mete out violence on the earth" can be applied to the leaders of Congress who fail to act to protect the people that have empowered them. It seems that their hearts, mouths, and actions are pursuing something other than justice for the American people. The word "mete" means to give out or measure. Both the rulers during David's day and ours issue decisions that result in grave injustices. Corruption persists, division continues, poverty thrives, and people continue to die. Just as David desperately needed God to intervene on behalf of His people, we too need a miracle.

"Break the teeth in their mouths, O God; Lord, tear out the fangs of those lions! Let them vanish like water that flows away; when they draw the bow, let their arrows fall short," he prayed (vs. 6-7). David pleaded for God to help; to purge the land of these wicked rulers. He recognized that as long as these individuals remained in positions of power that God's people would continue to suffer. David was tired of watching the rulers thrive and the people suffer. Has America grown sufficiently tired of its wicked leadership? Are you ready to do something yet?

Ecclesiastes 1:9 says "there is nothing new under the sun," which we have confirmed by reading Psalm 58. The frustration, anger, and righteous indignation that the godly feel for unjust leadership is a persistent human issue. What can we as the people of God do about it? First, seek God through prayer, asking Him to protect the righteous and judge the unrighteous. Second, we must speak up and fight against injustice. We are called to be imitators of Christ (Ephesians 5:1). Christ actively fought against the injustice of the leadership of the Pharisees and Sadducees. We cannot be "good Christians" and remain passive.

How can you respond to the unjust leadership around you in a way that imitates Christ?

Psalm 59

In this psalm, David prayed for deliverance when under attack. The first half of the psalm is spent in prayer and the second in words of faith that deliverance would come. This writing provides us with a good framework for approaching God about our needs.

The writer spends verses 1-7 talking to God about his problem. He obviously knew the truth of 1 Peter 5:7, "cast all your anxiety on him because he cares for you" because line-by-line he spelled out to God exactly what he needed and what was going on in his life. In verses 1 and 2, David asked for deliverance from his enemies. Then in verse 3, he began to tell his Heavenly Father what his enemies were doing to him, like a child returning home after being bullied at school. "They lie in wait for me," "I have done no wrong," "they return at evening snarling like dogs," "they spew out swords from their lips" (vs. 3-7). "Get them daddy," David exclaimed.

How do you tell God about your problems? David was open, honest, and spoke plainly. Do you dress up your concerns or gloss over them? Do you speak freely before God? "And when you pray, do not keep on babbling like pagans, for they think they will be heard because of their many words. Do not be like them, for your Father knows what you need before you ask him" (Matthew 6:7). God doesn't need to hear flowery words; He simple needs to hear your heart. Commit to stop all that rambling and just speak plainly to God today. If you were telling a friend about your problem what would you include in the story? Tell God who, what, when, where, why, and how? This is what David did; he walked God through his problem blow-by-blow without any pretense. Try it.

After David shared his situation with God, he began to express faith that God would help him. In verse 9 he said, "O my strength, I watch for you; you, O God, are my fortress, my loving God" and verse 17, "O my strength, I sing praise to you; you, O God, are my fortress, my loving God." Despite everything that his enemies were doing to harm him, David was confident that God would protect him, because God was his fortress. A fortress is a place of refuge and exceptional security, a stronghold, and defense. David not only held firmly to his knowledge of the character of God (for he knew God to be a refuge), but he also declared it.

Who is it that you know God to be? Speak it. Profess it. Confess it. The King James Version of Psalm 34:3 says, "O magnify the Lord with me, and let us exalt his name together." To magnify God is to increase Him, to make Him big in your eyes and life. When you speak about who God is, even before He has manifested those characteristics in your present circumstances, you shift your focus off of your problems and onto God. The bigger God is in our present, the less significant our present reality is, the less impact it has on our daily reality. Try it. Spend more time talking about God than your problem today; see what happens.

Psalm 60

Today, we read another lament attributed to David. He passionately expresses grief that God has rejected the people of Israel and suffered a military defeat as a result. Although David seems to spend a great deal of time complaining, crying out, and otherwise lamenting to God, I encourage you to be patient with him. David has been referred to as a man after God's own heart for a reason (1 Samuel 13:13-14). Much study and debate has been attributed to the reason why David was described in such a way, but I submit to you that all of his lamenting did not cut against his status, it actually contributed to it.

Although David had his issues, he had a very healthy relationship with God. David was in constant communication with God. With exception of the Bathsheba/Uriah fiasco, he consulted God prior to taking major action. In 1 Samuel 30:8 "David inquired of the Lord, "Shall I pursue this raiding party? Will I overtake them?" "Pursue them," he answered. "You will certainly overtake them and succeed in the rescue." Then David acted only in accordance with the Lord's command. As we studied in Psalm 32, David sought God's forgiveness when he messed up. David rejoiced before the Lord in 2 Samuel 6 when God returned the Ark of the Covenant to Jerusalem. We have seen him repeatedly express bold and confident trust in God during difficult times and entrust his enemies into God's hands as well. Displeasure, grief, and lament are apart of every genuine relationship. No one, including God, makes you happy ALL THE TIME. David understood what it meant to be in relationship with God and he took full advantage of it.

How real is your relationship with God? How genuine are you with God? David was not the only man who had an open and honest relationship with God; Jesus did as well. During the crucifixion Jesus cried out from the cross, "my God, my God, why have you forsaken me" (Matthew 27:46). Jesus was brutally honest with His Father about His feelings. Neither David nor Jesus was struck down by lightening for expressing himself openly to God and both of these men were highly regarded by God. In fact, God said of Jesus in Matthew 3:17, "this is my son, whom I love, with him I am well pleased." God desires an open and honest relationship with you.

Remember the words of James 5:13-17 today "Is anyone among you in trouble? Let them pray. Is anyone happy? Let them sing songs of praise. Is anyone among you sick? Let them call the elders of the church to pray over them and anoint them with oil in the name of the Lord. And the prayer offered in faith will make the sick person well; the Lord will raise them up. If they have sinned, they will be forgiven. Therefore confess your sins to each other and pray for each other so that you may be healed. The prayer of a righteous person is powerful and effective." God wants us to bring all of who we are to Him. He doesn't just want to fellowship with you during the good times of your life, He wants YOU, all of you, all the time. Tell Him ALL about whatever you are going through.

Psalm 61

Have you ever felt separated from God? Did it seem like no matter how much you prayed, worshipped, or praised that God was just beyond your reach? Did you feel as if you couldn't get close enough to truly feel His presence? David cried out in Psalm 61 to be restored into God's presence. He wept, "I call as my heart grows faint; lead me to the rock that is higher than I" (vs. 2). Although as followers of Jesus Christ nothing can separate us from the love of God, which does not mean that we will not *feel* distanced from His love or His presence.

"Your iniquities have separated you from your God; your sins have hidden his face from you, so that he will not hear" (Isaiah 59:2). While sin separates us from God, repentance brings us back to Him. Repentance requires us to look at our actions and life through God's lens. God asks us to turn and go in a different direction, the right direction, after we sin. The reward for doing so is reconnection with Him. The process of repentance begins with acknowledging that our conduct was sinful and then confessing that to God. "If we confess our sins, he is faithful and just and will forgive us our sins and purify us from all unrighteousness" (1 John 1:9). We are not only forgiven when we confess, but we are purified. Why does purification from unrighteousness matter? Our God is holy and calls us to be holy as well (1 Peter 1:15-16). It would seem impossible for sin and unrighteousness to stand boldly before a holy God. Repentance and the purification that comes along with it, removes the shame and guilt that sin bring.

Even when we have not been sinful, we may still experience feelings of separation from God. When hardship arises, we often ask ourselves "where is or where was God?" When struggling with difficult questions, we ask, "why isn't God speaking?" When struck with periods of loneliness, we ask, "why can't I feel God?" Although God promised to never leave us nor forsake us in Deuteronomy 31:6, that does not mean that we don't feel left or forsaken. David provides us with an excellent example in Psalm 61 of how to respond in these inevitable times. David reached out to God despite his feelings. In verse 2, he called out to God although he felt banished to the end of the earth. In verse

4, David asked to return to the sanctuary (the place where God dwells) and to be held in the wings of God. Finally in verse 7, he asked for permission to remain in God's presence forever. David did not allow his feelings of real or perceived separation from God to stop him from pursuing God.

If you feel separated from God persist in prayer. Deuteronomy 4:29 promises, "but if from there you seek the Lord your God, you will find him if you seek him with all your heart and with all your soul." David ran after God, even though he felt worlds apart from Him. Persist. Don't give up.

Psalm 62

This psalm reflects the simple trust that David had in God. I'm sure you've heard the expression, "It Ain't Deep." Trusting God was not a complex matter for David, he just did. Through all his tests and trials, it seems that he made up his mind to trust God and then acted upon that conviction. This is what we read in Psalm 62, when once again, David was confronted by the assaults of conspirators against him.

What are the convictions of your heart? What have you made up in your mind concerning God? Have you decided to trust God? David did and then wrote about it here. First, he confessed his trust in God (as evidenced by his ability to rest). Second, David shared his reason for trusting God. Following this writer's lead, write a statement of trust in God below:

Write a declaration to trust God (look at verses 1 and 2):

_____

_____

_____

_____

_____

Write a statement about your reason for trusting God (look at verses 5-7):

_____

_____

_____

_____

_____

David provides us with one more clue about the basis of his unquestionable faith and trust in God in verses 11 and 12. He says that he can trust God because of what God has spoken and what God has shown him. God had given David a word and had established a track record of being strong and loving towards

David. What has God told you? Promised you? Shown you? These are clues about your present reality and your future. If God has promised that you will own a successful business and your current one is closing, either it will be resurrected or you will start another. Have unwavering confidence in the Word of the Lord. If God has shown you that you will be happily married and your girlfriend has broken up with you, then trust God to have a plan to either bring reconciliation in that relationship or to unite you with the one that He is preparing for you.

David found rest in God alone, because he trusted in the Word and promises of God. Can you wait for the manifestation?

Psalm 63

According to the superscription (i.e. the prefatory language of the psalm), David wrote this psalm while he was in the desert of Judah, which means he was running from Absalom. He could have been sad or in despair, which I'm sure he felt at some point, but instead of getting stuck in those emotions, he chose to worship. David made a decision to confirm his faith in and love for God.

He began by expressing his desire for God. David was desperate for God and for closeness with God. He cried out, "O God, you are my God, earnestly I seek you; my soul thirsts for you, my body longs for you, in a dry and weary land where there is no water" (vs. 1). Although he had physical needs in the wilderness, his greatest need was spiritual. He hungered for God as if He were food and thirsted for Him as if water. David was keenly aware that only God could satisfy his needs. Is the same true for you? Do you know Jesus to be the bread of life? (John 6:25-59) Do you believe the promise of Jesus in Matthew 5:6 that those who hunger and thirst for spiritual food and drink shall be filled? Do you have a spiritual appetite that only God could satisfy?

What satisfies you? What do you find yourself being desperate for? The more I experience God, the more I want to experience God. The more I am in His presence, the more I want to be in His presence. Worshipping God created David's appetite for God. Verse 2 says "I have seen you in the sanctuary and beheld your power and your glory." It was through corporate worship that David had the type of encounters with God that he needed in this wilderness moment. Can you recall the moments when God touched you most deeply, healed your body, mind or broken heart, or gave you a peace that you couldn't begin to understand? Where were you? What was that like? Recalling these times of intimacy led David to long for them to reoccur and led David to offer God praise in a dark and difficult hour. "Because your love is better than life, my lips will glorify you. I will praise you as long as I live, and in your name I will lift up my hands" (vs. 3-4).

Diligent pursuit of God and reflection led David to a place of peace. He was able to lie down and rest comfortably (vs. 6). In God's presence, we find complete joy because all of our burdens become small when laid before a powerful and glorious God. Although the emotions of fear, doubt, insecurity, and disappointment were very real for David in this moment, he got past them by worshipping God. It was through worship that David was reminded that God was his help and would uphold him (vs. 6-8). With no one around, no instruments, or sacrifices to offer, David still worshipped and was encouraged to press on through the trial.

Encourage yourself today, by worshipping our awesome God.

Psalm 64

Reading this psalm lead me to remember a nursery rhyme that has become a school yard retort, "sticks and stones may break my bones, but words will never hurt me." There were many occasions when I would yell that back to another child if they said something mean to or about me, called me names, or otherwise used words to attack me. I have learned through experience, spiritual maturity, and Bible reading that this statement could not be any further from the truth. If you simply consider our study of the Psalms up to this point, David spends a great deal of time seeking the Lord about something his enemies said or the impact of their words on his life. Psalm 64 is no exception.

Let's look at some of the things that the Bible says about the tongue.

- Proverbs 18:21 "The tongue has the power of life and death."
- Matthew 12:37 "For by your words you will be acquitted, and by your words you will be condemned."
- Proverbs 15:4 "the soothing tongue is a tree of life, but a perverse tongue crushes the spirit."
- Proverbs 18:8 "The words of a gossip are like choice morsels; they go down to the inmost parts."
- James 3:6 "The tongue also is a fire, a world of evil among the parts of the body. It corrupts the whole body, sets the whole course of one's life on fire, and is itself set on fire by hell."

The words that we speak have a great impact. In Psalm 64, David describes the tongue of his enemies as a weapon (vs. 3-4). It is sharpened like a sword, aimed at its target like an arrow, and shot like a bullet. Have you ever been pierced by the words of another? In the same way that weapons can penetrate the body, words can reach deeply and impact our emotions and spirits. They impacted David so significantly that he requested of God "hide me from the conspiracy of the wicked, from that noisy crowd of evildoers" (vs. 2). David wanted the same type of physical protection that he requested in Psalm 59 when Saul sent men to kill him. Yes, sticks and stones can break our bones, but words can also hurt us tremendously.

Recognizing the impact of our words, how can you be a better steward of your words today? I implore you to try to apply the words of Colossians 4:6 to your speech today "Let your conversation be always full of grace, seasoned with salt, so that you may know how to answer everyone." Salt is a preservative and adds good flavor to food. In the same way, our speech is to be nourishing and life-giving.

Psalm 65

In this psalm, the writer gives God praise for His goodness to His people. He pours out thanksgiving for God's hearing and answering their prayers and recounts all the benefits they have experienced as a result. God has forgiven their sins and therefore they can continue to enjoy fellowship in the temple (vs.4). God has granted them protection and security in their land by protecting them from their enemies (vs. 5-8). God has also provided for their every need by taking good care of the land (vs. 9-13). God is good to Israel all the time and all the time, God is good.

How have you experienced the goodness of God in your life? What benefits do you experience because God has heard you prayer? Write a few of them here:

_____

_____

_____

_____

_____

_____

_____

David was an expert in repeating, rehearsing, and therefore remembering all God had done for him. Far too often, we find ourselves in distress and despair and then repeating past mistakes because of our limited ability to remember. Repeating and rehearsing the move of God helps prevent forgetfulness. When Israel was leaving Egypt, God told them to "remember this day" by celebrating the Feast of Unleavened Bread (Exodus 13). God wanted them to remember who God had been to them prior to leaving Egypt, so that they would not grow discouraged in the wilderness. But the people of Israel forgot and the consequences of their forgetfulness made a 40-day journey last 40 years. Commit to repeat, rehearse, and remember all that God has promised you and done for you today. "Be careful that you do not forget the Lord, who brought you out of Egypt, out of the land of slavery" (Deuteronomy 6:12).

Psalm 66

The writer of Psalm 66 invites the entire earth to join him in praising God. "Shout with joy to God, all the earth! Sing the glory of his name; make his praise glorious!" (vs. 1-2) David's praise is set in a context much bigger than himself and thanksgiving for the personal reasons that he has to glorify God. He recognizes that God is due praise from the entire earth. Today, I want us to think about the magnitude of God.

"In the beginning God created the heavens and the earth. Now the earth was formless and empty, darkness was over the surface of the deep, and the Spirit of God was hovering over the waters" (Genesis 1:1-2). Our God was there in the beginning and created everything out of nothing, as well as the potential to create everything that would ever be. From the very beginning, God created all things and beings with the ability to create and procreate. A God with that type of creating power is pretty awesome, right?! Who do you know with the power to create the earth? God did not just create one geographic area of the earth, but the ENTIRE earth. Asia, Africa, North America, South America, Antarctica, Europe, and Australia, were all God's handiwork. He even created the framework for those continents to sit upon. A God who can create the entire earth out of nothing and fill it with plants, water, air, sky, people and animals is worthy of praise.

God is not only big, but He does big things as well. "Come and see what God has done, how awesome his works in man's behalf!" (vs. 5-7) David called Israel to remember how God had delivered them from Egypt and parted the Red Sea so that they could cross. Just as God's creating power is worthy of praise, so is His saving power. David invites us to come and see God's saving acts throughout history by continually celebrating them through our praise. The Jews remember the Exodus from Egypt, and as Christians we remember the death and resurrection of Christ. "For God so loved the world that he gave his one and only Son, that whoever believes in him shall not perish but have eternal life. For God did not send his Son into the world to condemn the world, but to save the world through him" (John 3:16-17). Although all do not yet acknowledge Jesus and accept

Him as Lord, one day they will. Because Jesus died for all, we shall see the day when "all the earth bows down to you; they sing praise to you, they sing praise to your name" (vs. 4).

As a created being, as a saved being; I join my brother David and encourage you to "praise our God, O peoples, let the sound of his praise be heard, he has preserved our lives and kept our feet from slipping" (vs. 8).

God, our creator, is worthy of praise!

Psalm 67

Today, the psalm writer begins by asking God to bless Israel. Seeking God's blessing is not unfamiliar to us. We pray for God to bless us with good health, financial stability, success, and happy relationships. Ultimately, we all want the sun to shine on our street and divine favor to surround us. A blessing is a gift from God granted to us as an act of His grace; we do not deserve blessings. We cannot earn them. We are not owed them. We receive them only because God is great. Blessings are intended to glorify God, and help His people. God blesses us so that others will be blessed through us.

It is not about us! David understood this fact. After requesting that God bless the people of Israel, he stated his reason for the request "so that your ways may be known on earth, your salvation among all nations" (vs. 2). David wanted God's blessing as an evangelism tool. He desired that people know about God, understand His law, and personally accept Him as their God. Israel was not chosen to be God's people solely for their own benefit, but instead to be used by God. God wanted Israel to teach others about Him by being a nation of priests, prophets, and missionaries to the world. Israel was to be like a traffic sign, pointing people back to God. They were chosen, blessed, and set apart to help fulfill God's purposes in the earth.

Like Israel, God has chosen us. 1 Peter 2:9-10 says "but you are a chosen people, a royal priesthood, a holy nation, God's special possession, that you may declare the praises of him who called you out of darkness into this wonderful light. Once you were not a people, but now you are the people of God; once you had not received mercy, but now you have received mercy." We are not meant to be the sole beneficiaries of our salvation, but are called to draw people to God out of their darkness, despair, and sin. David understood his call to take God to the nations. But he also knew that he could not do it in his own strength, that he needed the blessings that come only through the supernatural move of God.

Check your motives today. Why do you ask God to bless you? How can you bless God by drawing others to Him?

Psalm 68

This beautiful Psalm of David focuses on the might of God. Our God has a robustly deep character. He is great and compassionate, loving and just, forgiving and judging, all at the same time. His might is among these character traits (i.e. strength, power, force, and valor). While our God is a lover, He is also a great warrior. It was the latter aspect of God's character that David focused on in this psalm.

This side of God has enemies (vs. 1), blows smoke (vs. 2), defends (vs. 5) and scatters kings (vs. 14). I can appreciate the question that disciples asked about Jesus in Matthew 8 when they said, "what manner of man is this?" As I read this psalm, I repeatedly thought, "I am glad that God is on my side." Our God is a bad dude! Not only is our God mighty, He does not travel alone. "The chariots of God are tens of thousands and thousands of thousands" (vs. 17). Our God is the Lord of Hosts; He has ultimate authority over every created thing. There is nothing or no one higher than our God. Now do you understand why Paul says, "If God is for us, who can be against us?" (Romans 8:31) God is mighty and leader of a great heavenly army, which He has the power to command to protect you.

There is a nugget tucked in this psalm that I don't want us to overlook. Verse 19 says, "Praise be to the Lord, to God our Savior, who daily bears our burdens." How does this verse fit in a psalm about the power, valor, strength and force of God? When we hear about God taking care of our needs it is usually in connection with the meek and mild, gentle and compassionate, mothering God, right? The writer is challenging our preconceived notions about God. To carry a burden requires strength, not weakness. Muscles are required. Generally, the stronger you are, the more you can bear. When we are called to cast our cares upon God, we are called to allow Him to assume/carry our load. God bears the burdens of the entire world, every single day. Can you imagine how heavy that weight is? But God effortlessly takes it on. That is some serious might. God uses His military power and strength to bear our burdens and to defeat our enemies. Hallelujah!

Whatever you are experiencing today, know that God is strong enough to carry it. Although your back and arms may be too weak to carry your lot, it is never too much for God. Give it to Him!

Psalm 69

Today, David cries out to God in anguish. He is experiencing a great deal of persecution and adversity. Unfortunately, this was a persistent theme of David's life. As much as David has come to be loved and respected by the generations of Jews and Christians that have followed him, if given the chance he would have likely traded places with any of us on any given day. David's life was hard. I would imagine that David could relate to Jesus' words in Mark 6:4, "a prophet is not without honor except in his own town, among his relatives and in his own home." David seemed to face more foes than friends, opposition than support, hatred than love, and battles than celebrations. Today, David stands as a pillar of the faith, but he paid an expensive price during his lifetime.

In our text today, David is being persecuted without reason (vs. 4). Have you ever faced meritless opposition? Did people speak against you without cause? Has anyone ever been determined to oppose your efforts, ideas, or call just because? Just because of their insecurity? Just because of their fear? Just because? My brother, my sister, you are in good company. This is the place that we meet David today; in the face of meritless opposition. David felt alone (vs. 8), mocked (vs. 10-12), and heartbroken and helpless (vs. 20). When he searched for comfort, he found greater attacks, opposition, and pain. Look at verses 20-21, "scorn has broken my heart and has left me helpless; I looked for sympathy, but there was none, for comforters, but I found none. They put gall in my food and gave me vinegar for my thirst." The word "gall" has several meanings, but in each case it refers to something bitter and disagreeable. Gall causes the skin to become irritated, swell, chafe, and abrade. When David cried out for help, his foes added insult to injury. David was kicked while he was down, salt was poured into his wombs, and his pain was turned into suffering. Have you ever been there?

Unfortunately, too many of us have set in David's seat. We've walked through valleys, experienced awful storms, endured sickness, sorrow, and sadness only to find that people responded with swords instead of arms of comfort. Fortunately, this was not the end of David's story, it wasn't the end of your story then, and it won't be the end of your story today. David pressed on. Verse 29 says, "but as for me, afflicted and in pain—may your salvation, God, protect me." He recognized that in the midst of his affliction and pain that God was there and would continue to be there. He knew that God would protect and save him from his trials, his pain, and his foes. God will save you too! There is no place that you can go to that will lead God to forsake you. Hebrews 13:5 says that God will never leave you nor forsake you, and God's Word is true. God will meet you in the heavens, depths, on the wings of the dawn, and on the far side of the sea (Psalm 139-8-9). Can you trust God to keep this promise?

Although David was in a bad spot, he decided to trust God. He decided to maintain his faith. David decided to resist despair. Don't miss that my brother, my sister—David decided. A decision is the act of making up one's mind. You too can make up your mind; you can decide. The choice is yours today. Decide to trust in the Lord. Decide to hope in the Lord. "Those who hope in the Lord will renew their strength. They will soar on wings like eagles; they will run and not grow weary, they will walk and not be faint" (Isaiah 40:31). The choice is yours.

Psalm 70

Today, David comes to God in desperation. He not only prays for a move of God, but also needs Him to move quickly. He cries out, "Hasten, O God, to save me" (vs. 1). Hurry God! As much as we try to "wait on God" and to trust His timing, there are occasions when it seems that we simply cannot endure the passage of time. Patience escapes us. Enduring is not a viable option. Tomorrow is too far away. Quite frankly, we need God to just come on with it. This is where we meet David in Psalm 70.

How many times have you found yourself in a déjà vu moment? Déjà vu literally means, "already seen" in French. We are said to experience déjà vu when we have the feeling that a current event or experience has happened before. David was probably having such a moment in Psalm 70, because he repeats his prayer from Psalm 40:13-16. This was the same old feeling all over again. "Be pleased, O Lord, to save me; O Lore, come quickly to help me. May all who seek to take my life be put to shame and confusion; may all who desire my ruin be turned back in disgrace. May those who say to me, 'Aha! Aha!' be appalled at their own shame. But may all who seek you rejoice and be glad in you; may those who love your salvation always say, 'The Lord be exalted.'"

As we have read in our study, David had all kinds of enemies and problems and experienced an array of emotions, over and over again. It is one thing to have a life threatening illness once, but cancer two times seems excessive. To lose one house to foreclosure is more than enough, but to lose the second to fire feels unfair. To have one major enemy is more than a notion, but two, three, or more...whoa! David was experiencing the same feelings again and cried out to the Lord, but had no new words to express this familiar sensation. He was sick and tired of being sick and tired. The prayer from Psalm 40 was tried and true. God responded the last time, so why chance this desperate time with something new? David went back to God with the words that worked before; save me! Except this time, David begged for God to move quickly.

How do you respond to repeated trials? What do you do when you are feeling the same pain, hurt, fear, doubt, or frustration from a prior season? Tried and true prayers work. God simply wants to know what you are feeling, what you need, and where you are—even if you have told Him before. His promise is still the same, "call to me and I will answer you and tell you great and unsearchable things you do not know" (Jeremiah 33:3). God will hear you and answer, even if it you pray the same prayer again and again.

What do you do when you are walking through a similar test or trial again?

Psalm 71

This anonymous psalm was written by one who was being pursued by his enemies and needed God's help and protection. This writer was obviously a believer and had been walking with the Lord for quite some time. Since birth he had been sustained by the Lord (v. 6), and in his youth he had been taught by the Lord (v. 17). In the midst of this trial, the writer reflected on his long lasting relationship with God. When you are discouraged, in distress, troubled or worried, try to reflect on your blessings and remind yourself of the faithfulness of the Lord. Although the psalmist was now in his old age, he knew that from conception to birth, and from birth to adolescence, the Lord had been with him. God was not about to abandon him now.

Through the course of his relationship with God, the writer came to know God as "his hope" (vs. 5). After reflecting over his past, he projected into the future that God would remain his hope; "I will always have hope; I will praise you more and more," trusting God to help him once again (vs. 14). Who has God been to you in the past that you need Him to be in your present and your future? Has He been your sustainer? Provider? Protector? Healer? Deliverer? Join the writer of Psalm 71 in making a bold declaration about who you will continually trust God to be. When we make these kinds of declarations, we become encouraged in the midst of our trials. Despite the current enemy attacks, the writer declared "you will restore my life again; from the depths of the earth you will again bring me up" (vs. 20). If God restored the life of the writer, He will also do it for you.

Even though God had not delivered the psalmist from this situation yet, he gave God praise anyway. The writer did not wait for the testimony, but started the praise party today. He pulled out his harp and lyre; opened up his mouth and lifted up the name of the Lord (vs. 22-24). Can you try that today? Praise God while you wait for Him to demonstrate His faithfulness to you, just as He has done many times before.

Psalm 72

Today, we meet Solomon, the son of David, who succeeded him as king. Here, he prays to the Lord for guidance and help in leading the people of Israel. Since these were the people of God, the king served as God's representative in the earth and therefore was required to align his leadership with God's law. Solomon knew that he could not lead the hardheaded Israelites without God's help, so he asked for all the characteristics that would help him rule in a manner pleasing to God; justice and righteousness (vs. 1), defense (vs. 4), endurance (vs. 5), diplomacy (vs. 10-11), concern for the marginalized (vs. 12-14), and the prayers of the people (vs. 15).

Far too many leaders fall short because they fail to realize what is required to be successful in their roles. It seems Solomon did not want to be one of those people, so he sought the Lord for guidance at the beginning of his reign. Not only did he need to align himself with God's law, he also had to be impartial in his dealings and ensure that his throne was built on righteousness and justice. In 1 Kings 3:1-15, God asked Solomon what he wanted as a coronation gift and he requested wisdom. God granted his request. A wise leader seeks God's guidance and endowment for the character, skills, and abilities required to fulfill his/her assignment. What role has God placed you in? What do you need to fulfill this assignment? Have you even asked God for help?

Proverbs 3:5-6 tells us to "trust in the Lord with all your heart and lean not on your own understanding, in all your ways acknowledge him and he will direct your path." Asking God to endow him to lead was an act of humility and surrender. Solomon not only acknowledges God as Lord of his life and throne, but also confessed his total dependence on God. The day that we begin to believe that we have everything under control is the day that we take our first step off of the path of God. "In their hearts humans plan their course, but the Lord establishes their steps" (Proverbs 16:9). We must remember that we have been placed in our respective roles, not for our own purposes, but for God's. Humility means to take a low view of one's own importance. Without humility, we can become hardheaded, stiff-necked, and pursue our own agendas. Commit to surrender your life, your role, and your agenda to God each day.

As Solomon continues to pray about his leadership, he begins to speak of the type of king that he desires to be. In verse 6, he says, "He will be like rain falling on a mown field, like showers watering the earth." Godly leaders are like the refreshing rain that makes the land fruitful and beautiful. We must be careful of our attitudes. One who refreshes, reinvigorates, revives, and brings life? Following a refreshing leader is a privilege and a delight. Submitting to their leadership is easy because they are such a joy to be around. But a leader with a bad attitude brings anxiety, frustration, and friction, which breeds opposition. Jesus was a refreshing leader. He spoke with compassion and love. He encouraged His followers to reach their potential. He led by example. Most significantly, He demonstrated a heart of humility and submission to the Father before the people. "Jesus gave them this answer: 'Very truly I tell you, the Son can do nothing by himself; he can do only what he sees his Father doing, because whatever the Father does the Son also does'" (John 5:19). As a leader, we should always seek to demonstrate the character of Christ; we should do what we have seen Christ do. When people see you, they should see Christ!

How can you surrender your role to God today? How can you lead with more humility?

Psalm 73

Today's psalm was written by Asaph. Like Korah, he was a Levite and served as a musician and worship leader at the sanctuary during David's reign. In this psalm, he ponders the age-old question of why the ungodly seem to prosper while righteous people suffer. How many times have you asked yourself, others, and even God that question? If I am one of God's faithful children, why am I broke, sick, lonely, despised, and otherwise going through, while THEY have not a care in the world? My hope is that after reading this psalm that you know that you are not alone. Although Asaph seems to be struggling with this reality, he transparently takes his questions to God. He may have been perplexed, frustrated, and discontent, but he knew where to take it--to God.

The first thing that we can learn from Asaph is to be brutally honest with God and ourselves about where we are, emotionally, spiritually, and mentally. In verse 2 he says, "but as for me, my feet had almost slipped; I had nearly lost my foothold." He came close to leaving the path of truth and standing firmly on the rock of godliness. This was no minor spiritual battle for Asaph, but instead it was an almost fatal trial of his faith. If your situation is bad, call it bad. If it is serious, call it serious. If it is scary, call it scary. It is only through truth that you will find freedom; "and you will know the truth and the truth will set you free" (John 8:32). Our ability to be honest with God is also a direct reflection of our trust in Him. "Trust in the Lord with all your heart and lean not on your own understanding; in all your ways submit to him, and he will make your paths straight" (Proverbs 3:5-6). Trust means to place your confidence, dependence, reliance, and hope in another person. Are you really trusting God if you withhold the truth from Him?

The second learning that we can take away from Asaph's trial in Psalm 73 is that we must be careful when and where we have temper tantrums. While Asaph asked a relevant and poignant question, "why the wicked thrive and the righteous suffer?" He did so by having a good 'ol fashioned, roll around on the floor, leg kicking, screaming and hollering temper tantrum. While he may have had a fit, he had it at home and not at the supermarket. Asaph demonstrated wisdom and maturity, even in the midst of a faith crisis. In verse 15 he says, "if I had said, 'I will speak thus,' I would have betrayed your children." Asaph recognized that as a worship leader, all eyes were on him. If he had publicly declared these thoughts, he could have caused others to slip. Even in the midst of our dark places, we have a responsibility to know when to express our brokenness and to whom. Asaph's faith trial could have been easily misinterpreted as faithlessness, giving up on God, or even blasphemy; all of which could have led God's baby sheep astray. Leaders must exercise wisdom.

Finally, we should learn the importance of keeping our eyes fixed on Jesus and not on other human beings. Focusing on the behavior of unbelievers led Asaph into the mess he was in; it will get us in trouble too. These people and the reality of their lives have no bearing on God's people. They live by different standards, if any. Serve a different master, if any. And have no heaven or hell to put us in. So why do we get caught up worrying about what they do, how they live, or how they prosper? Asaph almost gave up. He almost walked away from his leadership role and God because he erroneously decided to fix his eyes on the perceived prosperity of the wicked. Re-read verses 4-12, Asaph's account of the wicked is far from objective. Like Job, Asaph found himself in anguish focusing on the "good life" of the wicked (See Job 21). It was not until Asaph returned to the sanctuary and got back in the presence of the Lord that the mistakenness of his thinking was exposed (vs. 17). God has already made provision to deal with the wicked, so we need not be concerned with how they live (vs. 18-20). As for the righteous, we need to remain near to God (vs. 28) and fix our eyes on Jesus — the author and finisher of our faith (Hebrews 12:2).

Psalm 74

Today, we meet Asaph again. While he was crying out to God about a personal trial yesterday, today he is petitioning the Lord on behalf of all of Israel. This psalm dates back to the destruction of Jerusalem and exile of the people of Israel. The holy city was destroyed and the temple was no more. As you can imagine, the people of Israel desperately wanted God to come to their rescue and aid. They needed Jehovah Nissi (their banner) to defend them against their enemies.

It seems that Asaph believed that Israel was in this position because God had forgotten about them because the entire psalm is framed by his pleas for God to "remember." Repeatedly he tells God that "it was you" who acted in the past in order to drive home his point that only God could save them in the present. He reminded God of who He was and what He had done. He called forth God's kingship, reminded Him of His power to create, to defend, and rebuke; all of which Israel needed in the time of exile. This reminder served as both a source of encouragement and an expression of Asaph's faith. When we reflect on what God has been to us and done for us individually and collectively our focus shifts from our present trials back to God. We find hope while remembering who God is and what He has done. Although Asaph was calling God to remember, it was he that needed to reflect on those memories. God does not forget. "Can a mother forget the baby at her breast and have no compassion on the child she has borne? Though she may forget, I will not forget you! See, I have engraved you on the palms of my hands; your walls are ever before me" (Isaiah 49:15-17). Although God does not forget us, we forget Him and what He has done. "Be careful that you do not forget the Lord your God, failing to observe his commands, his laws and his decrees that I am giving you this day" (Deuteronomy 8:11).

Asaph needed to remember! What is it that you need to remember today? What is it that you need to call back up that God has done for you? Who has God been to you in the past that you presently need Him to be? Healer? Deliverer? Provider? Protector? Call it forth into your present!

Pray with me: *Gracious God, I thank you for all that you have been to me through the years. I bless you that before I knew you, you knew me and you were keeping me. I thank you for holding me back then and holding me now, in the palm of your hand. Bring back to my remembrance those times that you fed me with manna and quail from on high. Help me to recall each time you mended my broken heart. Remind me of the times that you opened doors that men and women wanted to close in my face. Show me the days that I could have perished, but you said no. Reveal to me the darts that you diverted. God, I need to remember you and the way that you love me, bless me, keep me, and hold me. I thank you that this time of remembrance shall bring hope and an increase in my faith. In Jesus name, Amen.*

Psalm 75

This psalm picks up where the last one left off. The writer seems to have remembered what God has been to and done for Israel. He has pressed his way beyond despair into a place of thanksgiving. After reciting the endless laundry list of all God had done in Psalm 74, the writer is so full of gratitude that he must share it with others. Asaph begins this psalm calling the people of God to give thanks and testify to all that God is and has done.

God interrupts him in the midst of his praise and thanksgiving to speak a word of reassurance. He says in verses 2-5, "I choose the appointed time; it is I who judge with equity. When the earth and all its people quake, it is I who hold its pillars firm. To the arrogant I say, 'Boast no more', and to the wicked, 'Do not lift up your horns. Do not lift your horns against heaven; do not speak so defiantly.'" Although Asaph had shifted to a place of thanksgiving, his situation had not changed. Israel was still in exile. Jerusalem was still destroyed. The prophets still weren't prophesying. Asaph's world was still spinning out of control, but God interrupted all of his confusion, frustration, and fear with a promise not to fail him or Israel. He promised to call their enemies to account.

God reminds Asaph that as bad as things may appear and as must terror as their enemies were bringing upon Israel, that He had a plan and was still in control. "Many are the plans in a person's heart, but it is the Lord's purpose that prevails" (Proverbs 19:21). It did not matter what their captors had in mind, God had preordained this exile and Israel's redemption. When God interrupted Asaph's thanksgiving He told him that He alone would choose the appointed time to judge the Babylonians, who held them captive, and He would do so in equity. Although all moral order seemed to crumble before the writer's very eyes, God would bring stability. "My God is my rock, in whom I take refuge, my shield and the horn of my salvation. He is my stronghold, my refuge and my savior-- from violent people you save me" (2 Samuel 22:3). Everything God had been to Israel in the past, He still was and would continue to be. As a pillar brings stability to a structure, God would bring stability to Israel.

God promised in Luke 20:43 to make your enemies your footstool. They will be steps that you can use to gain the leverage needed to propel you into your destiny, future, and purpose. Do you believe that? Do you trust God and the plan that He has for your life? Can you wait for the plan of God to unfold before your eyes? Although God promised to judge the Babylonians and to restore Israel, the people of Israel had to wait for several decades. God did restore Israel, but in His time. The people of Israel did leave Babylon. Jerusalem was rebuilt. The temple was restored. In God's time. My sisters and brothers, I encourage you to hold on to the promise of God; no matter how crazy it looks. "Wait for the Lord; be strong and take heart and wait for the Lord" (Psalm 27:14).

Psalm 76

Today we meet Israel, still in a bind. Still needing God to defend them and Jerusalem. The threat of danger and the presence of danger is a recurring theme in the life of the people of Israel. First, they fled from the Egyptians and then all of the tribes and nations in the wilderness. Next, came the Philistines. Followed by the Assyrians. All of this before they even got to the Babylonian exile. The Israelites were always running from someone or experiencing some sort of persecution. Our learning today comes not from the persistence of their enemy, but the persistence of their pursuit of God. Despite everything that happened around and to them, they persisted in seeking God for help, guidance, and deliverance. Psalm 76 was no exception.

Although Israel may have dreaded their enemies, their ultimate reverence was to God. "You alone are to be feared. Who can stand before you when you are angry?" (vs. 7) Asaph recognized that Israel's enemies had limited authority over them, while God's power was eternal. Why? Because they knew that God was in control of all things. Even though Israel found itself captive to the Babylonians, God was ultimately in control of their fate and destiny. For God is and was King of kings. "For dominion belongs to the Lord and he rules over the nations" (Psalm 22:8). Asaph ascribed all majesty and power to God, even above those that seemed to hold his life and the life of his people in their hands. Who is the boss of you? Is God in control or is another human being or system in control? Who determines your fate? "The Lord has made everything for its purpose, even the wicked for the day of trouble" (Proverbs 16:4, New Living Translation). Asaph recognized that even his enemies were subject to God. We must remember that Israel had turned aside from the Word of the Lord and refused to repent for these actions. God cautioned them that failure to do so would result in exile, so they were simply reaping what they sowed.

Even in the midst of judgment and God's wrath, He desires for us to place our faith in Him. No matter how bad your situation seems, trusting God and sticking with God is always the best option. Even if you got yourself into the situation, who other than God can bring you out? Asaph recognized this truth. "From heaven you pronounced judgment and the land feared and was quiet—when you, O God, rose up to judge, to save all the afflicted of the land" (vs. 8-9) God alone is judge and ruler of all the earth. He decides what is right and wrong. He alone can pronounce judgment and issue a pardon. I encourage you to seek God, even when you have done wrong. "Better is one day in your courts than a thousand elsewhere; I would rather be a doorkeeper in the house of my God than dwell in the tents of the wicked" (Psalm 84:10). Seek the Lord today!

Psalm 77

There are times in life that we are in really low places. We experience great pain, sorrow, suffering, or anxiety. These are times of distress, anguish, and even torture. No one can seem to fix it and nothing makes it better. Either someone has moved the exit from the valley that you are walking through or you are trapped there. This place of torment appears endless. This is where we meet Jeduthun (a descendant of Asaph) today…in his low place.

"I cried out to God for help; I cried out to God to hear me. When I was in distress, I sought the Lord; at night I stretched out untiring hands, and I would not be comforted" (vs. 1-2). The writer has done everything that he knows to do; he has prayed, fasted, read the scriptures, and sought Godly counsel, but he cannot seem to shake his sorrow. He found himself deeper in the pit than he realized or knew how to manage. Have you ever been there? What sent you there? Was it a divorce? An abusive relationship? A layoff? A death? What sent you on your downward spiral? Whatever caused Jeduthun to be in distress was not as scary as the fact that he could not find his way out. He was stuck. The more he reflected on who God had been in his past, the deeper it pulled him into his pit. "I remembered you, O God, and I groaned; I mused, and my spirit grew faint" (vs. 3). Have you ever sought God to execute the same miracle that He performed in a previous season to no avail? Instead of being encouraged by that time of reflection it only caused your faith to decrease, because for some odd reason God refused to manifest Himself in the same way? You are not alone. This is exactly where the writer was in Psalm 77.

But God! Instead of ceasing to reflect on God's previous goodness and miraculous acts, the writer forced himself to continue to reflect. Instead of retreating from the pain and running from the hurt, he ran towards it. He chose to go through instead of around. He went through the pain of remembering how God had delivered him before. He went through the pain of reflecting on God's mercy and grace. He went through the anger of God's unwillingness to comfort him in his present. Jeduthun courageously decided to face his pain and continue to remember. And he was rewarded. "Then I thought, "To this I will appeal: the years when the Most High stretched out his right hand. I will remember the deeds of the Lord; yes, I will remember your miracles of long ago. I will consider all your works and meditate on all your mighty deeds" (vs. 10-13). He chose to focus on God and His mighty acts instead of his situation and his emotions. His faith was strengthened and he was encouraged to hold on until God moved, as He had done so many times before.

Can you choose to go through the pain of God's silence instead of around it? There are so many other things and people that the writer could have turned to ease his hurt, but he chose to press through. He trusted God to lead him out of his distress, just as He had led Israel out of the bondage of Israel (vs. 20). Hold on. Face your situation. Trust God. He will move on your behalf and comfort you in the process.

Psalm 78

Today, we read a Psalm of Instruction where God warned Israel to avoid its past sins and to remember God's grace and covenant with them. The people of Israel are taken on a walk down memory lane. The writer tells of the covenant God made with their forefathers and how they turned their backs on God in return. They are reminded of how God delivered Israel from Egypt and how they grumbled and complained in return. The people's memories are refreshed about how God sustained them in the dessert, and how the people worshipped idols in return. This is one sad history lesson. God blessed and they cursed. God gave and they took. God loved and they rejected. Despite Israel's faithlessness and ungratefulness throughout history we see God's faithfulness, miracles, and grace.

A charge can be found in the midst of this familiar historical account. Verse 4 says, "we will tell the next generation." Israel is called to tell their history to their children, to share with the next generation. This is not a new call for Israel, because in Deuteronomy 6:4-9, after the Passover and the Exodus, they were given the Shema, which would become the foundation of their faith. "Hear, O Israel: The Lord our God, the Lord is one. Love the Lord your God with all your heart and with all your soul and with all your strength. These commandments that I give you today are to be on your hearts. Impress them on your children. Talk about them when you sit at home and when you walk along the road, when you lie down and when you get up. Tie them as symbols on your hands and bind them on your foreheads. Write them on the doorframes of your houses and on your gates."

The people of Israel were not only called to remember their history and how God had blessed them, but to pass it on to the next generation. Do your children, godchildren, nieces/nephews, cousins, students, and mentees know your faith story? Have you shared with them how and when God saved you? Healed you? Delivered you? Protected you? Verse 4 calls us to "tell the next generation the praiseworthy deeds of the Lord, his power, and the wonders he has done." Are you only telling your testimony to your peers or are you sowing seeds in the next generation? Your story is designed to strengthen the faith of others. "Then they would put their trust in God and would not forget his deeds but would keep his commands" (vs. 7). What you went through was not just about you, it was for the next generation to hope and trust in God.

Israel was not only charged with telling their history, but to share the commands of God as well. "He decreed statutes for Jacob and established the law in Israel, which he commanded our forefathers to teach their children so the next generation would know them" (vs. 5-6). The Shema called Israel to "impress them on your children." The Merriam-Webster dictionary defines impress as "to apply with pressure so as to imprint" and "to mark by or as if by pressure or stamping." Israel was called to brand their children with the commands of the Lord. When one is branded or tattooed, the message or image is permanently affixed to their body, becoming apart of them. Do you impress the Word of God on the next generation? Are you making sure that the scripture becomes a part of who they are?

We are called to pass down the commands of God so that our children and their children will remain faithful (vs. 8). "Start children off on the way they should go, and even when they are old they will not turn from it" (Proverbs 22:6). Are you doing your part to guide the next generation down God's path?

Psalm 79

Sometimes it really is too late. Israel was sent into exile because they refused to stop sinning. Israel persisted to sin, they failed to repent, and God sent judgment upon them. This punishment may seem harsh, but God continuously warned them over and over to stop sinning. Second Kings 17:7-23 explains exactly how Israel arrived at the place described in Psalm 79. It reads like a juicy blockbuster movie. God delivered Israel from the hands of Pharaoh. Israel did evil behind God's back; they worshipped idols. God got angry. The Lord warned them to stop sinning and to obey His commands. Israel refused to listen and continued to sin, followed other nations, and worshipped idols. "So the Lord was very angry with Israel and removed them from his presence" (2 Kings 17:18). Then God turned them over to their enemies. God gave Israel plenty of chances to get it right, but they persisted in sinning. Can you blame God?

We stand in the midst of God's judgment of Israel in Psalm 79 as Israel begs God to relent. They pray that God will see their remorse and release them from judgment. The generations that actually committed the sins that led to Israel's exile had died and a new generation stood before God wanting a clean slate. Israel wants mercy. Not only do they want mercy, but they also want God's protection from their enemies. They plead, "pour out your wrath on the nations that do not acknowledge you, on the kingdoms that do not call on your name" (vs. 6-7).

The writer raises a very interesting argument as to why God should help them. The writer believes that God's failure to grant Israel mercy is making Him look bad. "Help us, O god our Savior, for the glory of your name; deliver us and forgive our sins for your name's sake" (vs. 9). Quite honestly, I'm unsure what to think about the writer's reasoning. For the wrongdoer to say to the wronged, "Stop punishing me for what I did to you, because it is making you look bad" seems pretty self-centered. However, I must take a step back and consider context and culture at the time of the event. During that time, a nation's victory or failure was attributed to their god. The nation who was victorious was deemed to serve a stronger god. So, if the Babylonians persisted in destroying Israel then their god would be considered more powerful than the God of Israel. The writer of Psalm 79 knew that the God of Israel was not only mightier than the Babylonian idols, but also supreme. Moses used this same argument when he pled with God to forgive Israel of their sins in Exodus 32:12. God's reputation was at stake here!

As Christians, we represent God in the earth. We are God's ambassadors (2 Corinthians 5:20); His messengers; His officials. What we do and do not do points back to Jesus. How are you making God look? Are you glorifying God by the way you live your life? Are you an asset or liability to God's reputation?

Commit to be a worthy vessel and representative of God today by being obedient to His Word.

Psalm 80

Asaph continues his plea on behalf of God's people while in captivity today. Remember what we've learned thus far, the people of Israel persisted in sinning, God warned them to stop, Israel continued sinning, and God punished them by sending their enemies to carry them off into bondage.

Brief historical note: Prior to captivity, the people of Israel were divided into two kingdoms, Northern (Samaria) and Southern (Israel). This psalm speaks of the invasion of the Assyrians into the Northern Kingdom and hence the captivity of the tribes of Ephraim, Manasseh, and Benjamin. The fall of Samaria should have been a warning to people in the Southern Kingdom, who had not yet been invaded to start obeying the Lord, but we know the end of the story—Israel continued sinning.

By the time we arrive at Psalm 80, it seems that the people have learned their lesson. Asaph repeatedly begs for God's mercy. He requests that the Lord deliver His people from this crisis, although their unrepentant hearts got them in this bind. To repent means to "change one's mind"; to literally turn away from our sins, wickedness, wrongdoing, and indiscretions and go in another direction. Repentance requires a change in heart, such that one is sorrowful and regretful for their wrongdoing. Changing our mind requires us to think the same thing as God does about a matter. If God calls it sinful, you must call it sinful. If the Word of God says it is wrong, you concur that it is wrong. The heart and mind must join together for full repentance to occur. We cannot simply say we are sorry. We must be remorseful and act upon that remorse by changing our behavior. God tried to get Israel to repent of their sin for generations. They would apologize each time, but immediately resume their sinful behavior. In Psalm 80, it seems that Israel was ready to call sin sin, and to change their wicked ways. But it was too late...they were in bondage.

Take a moment to comb the walls of your mind and heart. Is there any sin hanging out there for which you have not repented? Ask the Lord to reveal the sin to you. Write those things down. One-by-one, pray the following prayer concerning each sin:

Gracious God, I come to you confessing the sin of _____ *[insert the sin specifically here]. I recognize that this sin is not of you and I desire to please you in my thoughts, words, actions and deeds. Forgive me, Lord. Help me to turn away from the sin of* _____, *because I do not desire to commit it again. Help me Lord to turn away from my sinfulness and to turn towards you. Show me how to remove this sin from my pattern of behavior, so that I can please you. In Jesus name, Amen.*

As humans, we are not strong enough to turn from sin on our own. It is only with God's help that we can truly repent. Proverbs 16:9 says, "in their hearts humans plan their course, but the Lord establishes their steps." Remain prayerful about these areas. Ask the Lord to direct your steps in a manner that is pleasing to Him and that helps you avoid your sin. Release yourself from any guilt or shame associated with the confessed sin. God has forgiven you, now you must forgive yourself and walk in freedom as God renews your heart and mind so that you can live out the change that you desire.

Psalm 81

Do you listen to God? Do you really listen? Verse 7 says "in your distress you called and I rescued you, I answered you." We call out to God and He answers, but do we hear and then do we will listen? This was the recurring theme of Psalm 81. Over and over God speaks through the writing of Asaph about how the people of Israel would not listen. Despite their hardheaded ways, God continued to purse the people of Israel. God begged His people to listen to Him. "If my people would but listen to me, if Israel would follow my ways" (vs. 13).

We often pray and pray and pray about a situation, but are we positioned to hear what God says? Israel was not in a position to hear God's words because they were disobedient and worshipped foreign gods (vs. 9). What could foreign gods do for Israel, for the Lord was the one who had kept them throughout their nation's history? He had brought them out of Egypt, sustained them in the wilderness, and was prepared to continue to supply all of their needs. "Open your mouth wide and I will fill it," God says in verse 10. But Israel stubbornly followed foreign gods, while still praying to the Lord for help. How backwards is that? Praying to one God for help and deliverance while practicing the ways of another, who does that? We do. We expect God to help us out of financial ruin when we followed the materialistic ways of American culture into the situation. We ask God to save our marriages when we allowed adultery to drive a wedge through our relationship. We ask God to bless us with fruitful careers when we pursued a job other than the one He was trying to lead us towards. I can go on and on about the various idols that we follow and listen to instead of the King of kings and the Lord of lords. What is distracting you from God today? What little idol is keeping you from hearing God?

The good news is that you can repent. You can change your heart and your mind and go in a different direction. God is pursuing you, just as He pursued the people of Israel. God wants you to listen to Him. I hear you my brother, my sister. You have been praying, right? But God isn't speaking. God says, "you will seek me and find me when you seek me with all your heart" (Jeremiah 29:13). Destroy the idols blocking the way and make a decision today to separate yourself from that which keeps you from submitting to the Word of the Lord and the Lord will answer you. It may not be in a thundercloud (vs. 7), but He will answer you.

Psalm 82

In this Psalm of Asaph, we find a cry for justice. Our God is just, meaning fair, righteous, right, and true. God called his kings, judges, and leaders in the Old Testament to reflect His character in the earth, including ruling with justice. One of the most significant tasks of a leader was to protect the powerless from exploitation and oppression. Among the powerless were the widows, orphans, poor, and politically weak. This call for justice carried over to the New Testament. Jesus said, "'truly I tell you, whatever you did not do for one of the least of these, you did not do for me'" (Matthew 25:45). God has called the Church/Body of Christ to care for the unfortunate and weak as well. Psalm 82 helps us to understand more about what God requires of us.

First, we must stop defending the unjust and showing partiality to the wicked (vs. 2). So many of our laws and systems have been set-up to protect the immoral, impure, and corrupt. We have written our tax codes and laws to protect the rich and powerful. We worship greedy and self-centered celebrities who glorify sex, drugs, and alcohol. We celebrate dysfunctional families, school systems, and communities. God is calling us to stop! "Woe to those who call evil good and good evil, who put darkness for light and light for darkness, who put bitter for sweet and sweet for bitter" (Isaiah 5:20). As followers of Christ, we are implored to call a spade a spade; to call wrong wrong and right right. "The righteous care about justice for the poor, but the wicked have no such concern" (Proverbs 29:7).

Second, we must "defend the weak and the fatherless; uphold the cause of the poor and the oppressed" (vs. 3). All the attention that we've put into defending the unjust, wicked, rich, and powerful should be shifted to the weak, fatherless, poor, and oppressed. God is calling us to take an active interest and stance concerning the "least of these." In order to defend these people, we must become aware of their presence, needs, and concerns. The Merriam-Webster Dictionary defines the word defend as "to drive danger or attack away from; to maintain or support in the face of argument or hostile criticism; and to attempt to prevent an opponent from scoring." God is calling us to advocate for laws and systems for the protection of the poor and oppressed, to block the arrows aimed at harming them, and to take proactive steps to support them. How can we do any of this if we are uninformed? How can you speak intelligently about that which you do not know?

Third, we must "rescue the weak and needy; deliver them from the hand of the wicked" (vs. 4). Not only are we called to defend them with our words, votes, advocacy, and a restructuring of our systems, we are charged with rescuing and delivering them. If a man falls overboard while sailing on a ship a lifesaving device of some sort is usually thrown to him in the water. In some cases, a raft or another boat is sent to the place where he is located. All of these mechanisms are used to pull that individual out of the water. God is charging us to not only care and speak up for the least of these, but to take active steps to help pull our brothers and sisters out of lowly positions. As God's arms and hands in the earth, we are tasked with strengthening the weak, mothering and fathering the orphans, carrying for the widows and helping the poor to rise above their position.

What steps do you need to take today to respond to call of Psalm 82? How will you defend, rescue and deliver our brothers and sisters today?

Psalm 83

We learn a very important lesson through this Psalm of Asaph today. The ultimate purpose of God's warfare is not about us. Yes, God defends us because we are His children and He loves us dearly. Yes, God desires that we be secure. However, the ultimate goal when subduing our enemies is worldwide acknowledgment that God "alone [is] the Most High over all the earth" (vs. 18). The King James Version of Second Peter 3:9 states that God does not will that "any should perish, but that all should come to repentance." He wants every person on this earth to turn from his or her current ways, ideology, and beliefs and turn towards serving Him and Him alone. Period. It is just that simple.

Asaph goes through a pretty lengthy recitation of all of Israel's enemies and their attempts to wipe Israel out. This is followed by a detailed description of how Asaph would like for God to handle them. The most compelling reason for God to move does not come until verse 16; "cover their faces with shame so that men will seek your name O Lord." What is the basis for your requests for God to pursue your enemies? Is it about you or about God? Asaph recognized that if Israel's enemies were victorious that God would not be glorified. During biblical times, the victory, success, and prosperity of a nation ascribed to the god of the successful nations. Likewise, defeats, failures, and poverty were deemed a result of the weakness of a nation's god. Aspah refused to allow his God to be seen as anything other than the Most High God.

I implore you to remember that it is not about you today. It is about God. It is about people coming to know God, worship God, and serve God. We are led and guided for God's namesake (Psalm 31:3). We receive God's mercy for God's namesake (Ezekiel 20:44). We are defended against our enemies, for God's namesake (Jeremiah 14:7). We serve the Lord, for God's namesake (3 John 1:7). Prior to petitioning the Lord; I challenge you to ask yourself "is this request for His namesake?" If God grants my request, will it bring Him glory?

Psalm 84

As we read this Psalm of the Sons of Korah (descendents of the Levitical line of Korah) the writer's delight for God and the things of God jumps off the page. Specifically, he adores the Lord's temple (vs. 1) to the point of longing to dwell there. He writes, "my soul yearns, even faints for the courts of the Lord; my heart and my flesh cry out for the living God" (vs. 2). During Old Testament times, the temple was where God resided. Hence, entering the temple meant access to the presence of God. The writer did not have free access to the temple of the Lord, and was envious of those people and creatures that did. He was jealous of the birds that built nests in the temple near the altar (vs. 3). He longed to be among the pilgrims traveling to the temple (vs. 5). This writer's love for God's temple and yearning to be in God's presence is so great that he'd rather be a humble servant at the temple than hold a high position at the tents of the wicked (vs. 10).

Do you love the house of the Lord? Do you long to attend worship service, Bible study, or even meetings/rehearsals? Is the presence of the Lord so significant to you that you are desperate to get to the place where He dwells?

Unfortunately, many of us have no context for this psalm writer's perspective. We can enter the church whenever it is open, because nothing is restricting our access. Even when we travel and are incapable of getting to "our" church, we can attend service somewhere else. This Son of Korah lived during a time when there was only one temple. One place where God dwelled. One place to access the presence of God. One place where sacrifice could be made. One place where sins were forgiven. He lived under the old covenant where a high priest stood between him and God. His access to God, even when he could make his way to the temple was hindered. As Christians, this is a foreign concept. Jesus reconciled us to God so that we would never be separated from God (2 Corinthians 5:18). We have the presence of God living inside of us through the precious Holy Spirit who leads and guides us (John 14:25-26). Christians make up the Body of Christ, hence it is impossible for us to be disconnected from God (1 Corinthians 12:27). No matter where we are geographically or physically located, we ARE the Church! As a result, we can freely enter God's temple and approach His altar with unhindered access (Hebrews 4:16). But do we appreciate this freedom? Do we see this as a privilege?

"For I am convinced that neither death nor life, neither angels nor demons, neither the present nor the future, nor any powers, neither height nor depth, nor anything else in all creation, will be able to separate us from the love of God that is in Christ Jesus our Lord" (Romans 8:38-39). I challenge you to spend some time thanking God for the privilege of unhindered access to God and His temple. Ask the Lord to renew your adoration for Him and His Church.

Psalm 85

Today's psalm provided one of the most beautiful and compelling images of the benefits of God's salvation. Re-read verses 9-13. Did these verses electrify you? I am excited about the promise found in this text. "Surely his salvation is near those who fear him, that his glory may dwell in our land" (vs. 9). Wherever God's saving power is manifested, His glory is also revealed and resides. Each time a person is saved, God's glory reaches to the place where they are and it remains there. Recall that to "dwell" means to remain, reside, and stay. So when we are saved, God's glory comes upon us and stays with us. We have been marked by the glory of the Lord! Hallelujah! God's glory is synonymous with honor, praise, splendor, worthiness; the overall manifestation of God's greatness. Good God almighty! You my sister, my brother, have been marked with the manifestation of God's greatness. The glory that we have received does not leave us, unlike the cloud by day and the fire by night through which God manifested His glory to the Israelites as they wandered through the wilderness. Eventually, the cloud and fire left them. But God's glory remains with us.

"Love and faithfulness meet together; righteousness and peace kiss each other" (vs. 10). Although this is beautiful poetry, it is also a personification of God's gifts to those He saves. When we are saved, we join God's covenant people and are blessed with God's unmerited favor. The writer of Psalm 85 identifies love, faithfulness, righteous, and peace as evidence of God's favor. As God's people, He lovingly relates with us. He faithfully cares for us. In righteousness He leads and guides us. And He bestows upon us perfect peace. It is awesome to serve a God with such impeccable character.

As God manifests His favor towards us through His love, faithfulness, righteousness, and peace, He models for us how we are supposed to deal with one another. We are called to walk in the same love, faithfulness, righteousness, and peace that God shows us. It is only through Christ that we obtain these Godly characteristics and demonstrate them in our relationships, but we can do it! "I can do all things through Christ who strengthens me" (Philippians 4:13). Receiving the favor of God's blessings changes us and changes the world; "faithfulness springs forth from the earth, and righteousness looks down from heaven" (vs. 11). All of creation is shifted as we demonstrate God's character.

Ask God to help you to manifest His love, faithfulness, righteousness and peace in all your relationships today.

Psalm 86

David is back! And he is being attacked by his enemies, once again. David did what David does, he ran to the Lord for help. "Hear, O Lord, and answer me, for I am poor and needy" (vs. 1). He humbly recognized that he was in a desperate position and he told God about it. Then David told God exactly what he needed; he cried "guard my life" (vs. 2). Next, David reveals a bit about himself. Despite his desperation, David is confident. Not in his own ability, but in God. "You are forgiving and good, O Lord, abounding in love to all who call to you...In the day of my trouble I will call to you, for you will answer me" (vs. 5, 7). David knows that God will answer his prayer. Period.

We can learn something from our brother David's confidence. We often go to God timidly, unsure, and even doubtful that God can or will answer our prayers. Why is that? Hebrews 4:16 tells us to "approach God's throne of grace with confidence, so that we may receive mercy and find grace to help us in our time of need." Some translations say for us to go "boldly" to the throne. That means fearlessly, courageously, and confidently. What are you afraid of? David asked for what he needed and placed his trust in God's willingness and ability to respond. We often hedge in our prayers. Praying things like "if it be your will," "if you are willing to," "if you might." Either God is Lord of your life or He is not. Either you believe the promises of His Word or you don't. Either God is going to do it or He is not. Hedging only interjects doubt, fear, and distrust into our prayers. Commit to stop it, today! "If you believe, you will receive whatever you ask for in prayer" (Matthew 21:22). I hear your brain turning. What if what I'm asking for is contrary to God's will? Then you won't get it. God is not going to act contrary to His will. Period. But God will respond to your prayer even if the response is to tell you no. "But when you ask, you must believe and not doubt, because the one who doubts is like a wave of the sea, blown and tossed by the wind." (James 1:6).

Trust God today. Get Honest. Get Bold. Watch God move. "Ask, and it will be given to you; seek, and you will find; knock, and it will be opened to you" (Matthew 7:7).

Psalm 87

The writer of Psalm 87 refutes any belief that God does not desire for all persons to be saved and to join the ranks of His people. If we somehow overlook 2 Peter 3:9, "The Lord is not slow in keeping his promise, as some understand slowness. Instead He is patient with you, not wanting anyone to perish, but everyone to come to repentance," and 1 Timothy 2:3-4 "this is good, and pleases God our Savior, who wants all people to be saved and to come to a knowledge of the truth," Psalm 87 brings the plan of God back into view. God wants all of His creation redeemed and hence saved.

The psalmist celebrates Zion (Jerusalem) as the city of God and the object of His love. Jerusalem was founded by God to be the holy city; the place where He would rule over His people. The place where God would dwell among them in His temple. This is the reason that Zion is God's most cherished city among all of the lands occupied by the people of Israel (vs. 2). Since this is God's dwelling place, it makes sense that He would call all nations and tribes to worship there.

In verse 4, the writer names various Gentile nations that would be saved and join the people of Israel in worshipping God. The psalm foresees widespread conversion of all people; Rahab (Egypt), Babylon, Philistia, Tyre, and Cush. These nations represent people from all over the world who would come to acknowledge the God of Israel (vs. 4) and join their voices with Israel singing worship to Yahweh (vs. 7). Although each of these nations had been hostile towards God and His people at one point in history, God still had plans to redeem them. Isn't this great news?! Even those people who position themselves as enemies of God can repent and be saved.

God is still on a mission to redeem all of creation. He still wills that all people be saved. The vision set forth in Psalm 87 is yet to be fully realized. But the day will come and we will see at the end of time, the prophesy of this scripture and Revelation 7:9 realized, "After this I looked, and there before me was a great multitude that no one could count, from every nation, tribe, people and language, standing before the throne and before the

Lamb. They were wearing white robes and were holding palm branches in their hands." Getting there is not only up to God. Just as God wanted to use Israel to bring people to Himself, He desires to use us. When Jesus was ready to depart this earth He gave His followers marching orders to partner with God in His work of redemption. In Matthew 28:19-20, Jesus commanded us to "go and make disciples of all nations, baptizing them in the name of the Father and of the Son and of the Holy Spirit, and teaching them to obey everything I have commanded you. And surely I am with you always, to the very end of the age."

We are called to take God and His Word to all nations. Then we are commanded to teach people everything we know and how to obey the commands of God. What are you doing to help bring people to God? How are you living out the command of Christ? Now what can you commit to doing today to become an active participant in God's redeeming work?

Psalm 88

The writer of this psalm cries out to God from the depths of his being. He has been on the edge of death his entire life. He exclaims, "from my youth I have been afflicted and close to death" (vs. 15). Most of us have had experiences that could have ended in death, be they car accidents or illnesses; unfortunately, this writer seems to have experienced them over and over again. He has lost his strength (vs. 4), he is dying (vs. 5), his friends are gone (vs. 8), and he can't escape his current situation (vs. 8).

This psalm illustrates one of the realities of God's people, which few people want to discuss. Godly people are not exempt from trials. Yes, people of faith can live lives of constant, incessant, recurring trouble. Our faith and service of God does not keep us from illness, broken hearts, enemy attacks, financial trouble, or other disastrous realities. The saints go through!

Many people often ask me, what is the point? Why serve God and be faithful, if I am going to experience life's hardship anyway? Although no person is exempt from "life happening" something is different between an unbeliever and a believer going through a storm. When talking about believers who have died, Paul tells us in 1 Thessalonians 4:13, "you do not grieve like the rest of mankind, who have no hope." God's people have hope in the midst of the trial. Why? The writer of Psalm 88 tells us in verse 1; we serve the "God who saves." When we go through, we can grasp this hope. We are able to confidently expect a brighter day, a change in our circumstance, peace of mind, healing in our bodies, relief from pain, and a myriad of other results. Even if God has willed for us to die, we know that we will be with Jesus on the other side of death.

It is because of this hope that this psalm writer persisted in prayer, despite his distress. In verse 9 he writes, "I call to you, O Lord, every day." He prayed without ceasing, despite his circumstance. Although he felt rejected (vs. 14), he continued to cry out to the Lord. Because he knew that God was his Savior (vs. 1). If anyone could help him, it was God.

Where is your hope placed? In whom do you trust?

Psalm 89

Today, we face another hard question; does God break His promises? We have all heard that God, in fact, keeps His promises, that God does not lie or change His mind. There are even scriptures that support these premises. Deuteronomy 7:9 says "Know therefore that the Lord your God is God; he is the faithful God, keeping his covenant of love to a thousand generations of those who love him and keep his commandments." Numbers 23:19 "God is not human, that he should lie, not a human being, that he should change his mind. Does he speak and then not act? Does he promise and not fulfill?" Isaiah 55:11 "So shall my word be that goeth forth out of my mouth: it shall not return unto me void, but it shall accomplish that which I please, and it shall prosper in the thing whereto I sent it" (King James Version) But in today's text, Ethan wants to know why he is facing his current situation if the Word of God is true. God promised David in 2 Samuel 7 an eternal dynasty, but by the time this psalm was written Israel was in bondage, the temple was destroyed and they had no king (let alone a Davidic king) on the throne.

Ethan spends verses 20-37 reminding God of the words of His promise, as if God had forgotten. "No enemy will subject him to tribute" (vs. 22), "my faithful love will be with him and through my name his horn will be exalted" (vs. 24), "I will maintain my love to him forever, and my covenant with him will never fail." (vs. 28) Ethan cries out "God what happened?" Have you ever felt like Ethan? As if God failed to keep a promise that He made to you? If so, you're not alone! Most of us have been there and will go there again.

Let me remind you of two things, 1) as humans, our perspective is quite limited (i.e. we only have a portion of the information); and 2) God is sovereign. Isaiah 55:8-9 says, "'for my thoughts are not your thoughts, neither are your ways my ways,' declares the Lord. As the heavens are higher than the earth, so are my ways higher than your ways and my thoughts than your thoughts." God wrote the master plan. He knew how things would start and end from the very beginning of time and therefore He is privy to some things that we are not. "And we know that in all things God works for the good of those who love him, who have been called according to his purpose" (Romans 8:28). God not only wrote the plan, but He is working the plan. He is the creator of the puppets, the writer of the script, and the puppeteer who is making the puppets perform. So God is making ALL THINGS, that means the entire plan for all beings (not just you), work together to fulfill His ultimate plan. He can do as He chooses, when He chooses, and how He chooses. BUT, God does not lie or break His promises.

We know the end of Ethan's story, but Ethan did not. He was too close to the situation to appreciate that God was disciplining Israel, as He said He would for their unfaithfulness. Ethan did not know that God was sending Jesus through the line of David to be the King of kings and the Lord of lords. While David's life was limited and therefore his ability to rule was limited by life and death, his descendant Jesus "[would] reign over Jacob's descendants forever; his kingdom will never end" (Luke 1:33). Ethan's ability to understand the promise of God and how it would be manifested was limited. But the God Ethan served and the God we serve is infinite and so is His plan. Our understanding is limited by time, space, and matter, but we serve an unlimited God. The next time you feel that God has broken His promise to you, remember 1 Corinthians 13:12 "For now we see only a reflection as in a mirror; then we shall see face to face. Now I know in part; then I shall know fully, even as I am fully known." You are seeing only part of the picture. Besides, God has all eternity to fulfill His promises. Wait an eternity before you call Him a promise breaker.

Psalm 90

The superscription of this psalm refers to this as a "prayer of Moses the man of God," not because Moses authored it, but because it is written in the spirit of Moses. It sounds like a prayer Moses would pray. Why? Some of the words from Deuteronomy 32 and 33, which have been attributed to Moses are duplicated here. Moses was also constantly interceding for the people of Israel as they wandered through the wilderness on their way to the promise land. The writer of this psalm prays passionately for the eternal God to have compassion on His sinful people. Like Moses, he begs for God to withhold His wrath after the people of Israel messed up once again.

In the midst of this plea for mercy is a wonderful comparison of the boundless nature of God and the limitedness of humans. "Before the mountains were born or you brought forth the whole world, from everlasting to everlasting you are God" (vs. 2). Before the earth was created, God was God. Prior to the existence of any animal, plant, or human being placed on the earth, God was God. When there were no continents, God was God.

Look around the space where you are sitting at this very moment. What do you see? Name some of things that you see. Look down at your self. Now close your eyes. Mentally erase each of those things, one by one, from your minds eye. Lastly, erase yourself. There is nothing but black space, right? When all that existed was black space, God was God. "In the beginning God created the heavens and the earth. Now the earth was formless and empty, darkness was over the surface of the deep, and the Spirit of God was hovering over the waters" (Genesis 1:1-2).

God was God when everlasting began and the same will be so when everlasting ends. God is not bound by time, space, or matter, because God is eternal. God's eternal nature allows Him to be Israel's "dwelling place throughout all generations"; God has been there for them through it all. Unlike God, the life of a human is fleeting. "The length of our days is seventy years or eighty, if we have the strength" (vs. 10). We come from the dust that God created and to that same dust we also return (vs. 3). God lives forever.

Not only is God eternal, but He is also Lord (vs. 1). This means that God has power, control, and authority over the territory and people under His jurisdiction. Since God created all people, places, and things, He has sovereign authority over all of creation. God's authority extends throughout the world and covers the universe. God is the decider of all! Get this... Since God is sovereign and eternal, He is the decider over all things FOREVER. He decided yesterday. He decides today. He decides tomorrow.

Since God is both sovereign and eternal, He controls time and what occurs within time. This includes our life span. God decides just how fleeting our lives on this earth will be. "Yet you sweep people away in the sleep of death — they are like the new grass of the morning: In the morning it springs up new, but by evening it is dry and withered" (vs. 5-6). Whether we are here today and gone tomorrow is ultimately up to God. There are instances when this truth is difficult to understand and face, but the complexity of this reality does not change its nature — it is still true. God is in control. Even when some seem to die too young or others die tragically, God is still God and His plan is much bigger than ours. "'For my thoughts are not your thoughts, neither are your ways my ways,' declares the Lord. 'As the heavens are higher than the earth, so are my ways higher than your ways and my thoughts than your thoughts'" (Isaiah 55:8-9). Our finitude prevents us from seeing beyond our current reality, but God has an eternal view. Place your trust in His eternal and sovereign plan and find rest for your soul.

Psalm 91

Today, we have the testimony of one who chose to place his trust in God. Although yesterday we read about the limits of humanity, today we learn that there are rewards for those who faithfully lean into the limitlessness of God. These rewards are significant and abundant.

When we stay in the shelter or persistent state of protection of God we find:

1. **Rest-** our minds, hearts, and souls are quieted so that the Spirit of God can envelope and permeate us; all of our concerns cease to afflict us.
2. **Refuge-** we enter a place of safety where we find hope, shelter, and trust.
3. **Protection from Danger-** The fowler's snare is a metaphor for danger from human enemies; we are protected from the attacks of enemies, known and unknown.
4. **Covering-** God sends forth His power to shield us from the storms of life like a mother bird hiding her babies from the rain and vicious predators.
5. **Faithfulness-** "Never will I leave you; never will I forsake you" (Hebrews 13:5). God will always be there and keep his promises.
6. **Fearlessness-** we can live without fear because God will protect us and keep us safe 24/7; it does not matter when the attack comes,
7. **Guarding-** not only will God protect us, but also He will send guardian angels to protect us and watch over us and everything we do.
8. **Redirection Out of Harms Way-** if we find ourselves in harms way, God's angels will lift us up above the threat; not even our foot will be harmed by trouble (vs. 12).
9. **Victory-** when God sends us into battle, we will win. All the forces of evil that attack us will be under our feet (vs. 13).
10. **Honor-** we will be glorified, made great, and promoted.

11. **Long Life**- although human life is fleeting (as we learned in Psalm 90), this is how we receive the strength we need to endure (Psalm 90:10).
12. **Salvation**- even when our life on earth has ended, we will live eternally with God.

My charge to you today is to dwell. Choose to dwell "in the shelter of the Most High" (vs. 1). You have a lot to gain by doing so. The rewards of God await you. Tap into this place of rest and security. God will not disappoint you. What do you have to lose?

Psalm 92

The Word of God repeatedly calls us to praise, pray, and worship. If we were honest, I mean really honest, we would have to admit that there are times that we do not know what to say to God. Whether it is because the circumstances of our lives are consuming us, because we are distracted by our thoughts, we are too emotional, or simply are lost for words; the Psalms are often helpful. The writer of Psalm 92 gives us insight about some of the ways and methods that we can praise God.

"It is good to praise the Lord and music to your name, O Most High" (vs. 1). We can sing a song from our hearts, play the piano, drums, guitar, or string instruments for God. One of the Hebrew words for praise is "halal," which means to celebrate, glorify, and boast about God. Another word for praise is "yadah" which means to give thanks. Praising God is simply about lifting up the name of God. Making music is simply one method of praise. Don't worry; we do not have to be musically inclined to praise God through music. God loves to hear our music in praise, no matter how flat or off-key our voices may be. If creating music is out of the question for you, then sing the hymns of the faith or praise choruses that express your heart. Sincerity of the heart in praise is what God desires.

Verse 2 says to "proclaim your love in the morning and your faithfulness at night." Wake up in the morning and glorify God for His love towards you. How has God demonstrated His love for you in the past? How is He doing so in the present? Has He kept you safe? Has He comforted you? Has He given you breath? Has He been there for you? Sing about it. Dance about it. Write about it. Thank God for it.

We are in relationship with a living God--a God who can see and hear and touch and feel. Our God has emotions. Just as you like to hear the reasons why people love you, so does God. Tell Him. Show Him. Then praise Him for His faithfulness. We serve a trustworthy and reliable God. A God who does not break His promises.

Praise is such an important part of our communication with God. Glorifying God is the least we can do for all that He is to us and has done for us. When you find yourself at a lost for words or your praise becomes too routine and familiar, search the Word for new ways to lift up the name of our Savior. God is waiting to hear from you.

Psalm 93

Yesterday, we talked about some approaches to giving God praise. Today, the psalmist provides instruction on the content of our praise. The writer spends some time focusing on WHO God is to Him and creation.

1. **God is the reigning king over the entire universe.** He has authority and dominion over all of creation. He rules. He governs. He controls.
2. **God is mightier than any other god.** God has demonstrated His strength, power, and force since the world was created. He has shown Himself to be greater and bigger than any other force or any other god. Nothing surpasses Him. This includes the forces of nature, which bow to God's commands.
3. **God is eternal.** There was never a time that He was not; and there will never be a time that He does not exist.
4. **God is stable and reliable.** "For the mouth speaks what the heart is full of" (Luke 6:45). Since God is faithful, His Word, commands and statutes are as well. "Every word of God is flawless; he is a shield to those who take refuge in him" (Proverbs 30:5).
5. **God is holy.** God is pure, flawless, sinless, and without defect.

The attributes of God are factual. They are truth. Regardless of whether society chooses to accept them or not, they are true. God is King. God is mighty. God is eternal. God is stable and reliable. God is holy. When we profess truth about God, we honor Him, praise Him, and glorify Him.

God has called for praise from His creation. What truths about God can you profess today? Who has God shown Himself to be in your life?

Psalm 94

The writer of this psalm asks the Lord to vindicate the weak from the wicked, powerful, and arrogant. He calls upon the Lord as judge of the earth, to bring a stop to their arrogant words (vs. 4), oppression (vs. 5), and murder (vs. 6). The writer is not only inflamed by the harm inflicted upon the powerless, he is also outraged at the disrespect of God who hears and sees all the wrong being committed (vs. 9) and even knows the wicked thoughts of the perpetrators (vs. 11).

The psalmist shifts his focus in verse 12. Instead of continuing to concentrate on the wrongdoing of the wicked, he begins to see the blessings upon the righteous. "Blessed is the man you discipline, O Lord, the man you teach from your law; you grant him relief from days of trouble till a pit is dug for the wicked" (vs. 12) Yes bad things are happening to the righteous, but there is good news—they are blessed. Notice that the writer did not say that God is still blessing or bestowing blessings upon the righteous but instead that they "are blessed." A blessing is an act or thing. To bless is to give or bestow an act or thing. However, the word "blessed" refers to a condition or state of being. Receipt of a blessing or the act of blessing is potentially a one-time occurrence, while blessedness is an ongoing condition or state of being. Righteous people live in a state of blessedness. The Hebrew word used for blessed in this text means happy. Yes, although the people of God are going through hell and high water, they are happy!

As we go through trials and tribulations we are strengthened by the discipline of God. The word disciplined in this text refers to teaching and instruction from the law of God. The psalmist recognized that the challenges of life have the ability to help us to grow and mature in the faith, which draws us closer to the Word of God. The more we read God's Word, the more we know about God, His plans for us and the life He has destined for us. We are strengthened as we read the Word. We are not only equipped with the knowledge and understanding we need to withstand our current battles, but to also overcome future ones.

God disciplines us/drives us to His Word through our trials, because He loves us and wants us to grow-up in the faith. "For whom the Lord loves He chastens" (Hebrews 12:6, King James Version). God uses tests, trials, and other personal difficulties to grow us up. God desires that we become mature, attaining to the full measure of Christ so that we will not be tricked or deceived by false teaching and bad doctrine (Ephesians 4:13). Although we would like for things to be easy, we learn best through difficulty. Why? Adversity drives us to the Word and to God.

The wicked will get their day. Try not to focus on their wrongdoing, but instead ask God "what are you trying to teach me? What truths do I need to understand about you and your plan for me?" God has great plans for you, but you have to be prepared to possess them. Your trials are your training ground. Thank God for your training today.

Psalm 95

The psalmist continues teaching us about the way to praise and worship God in Psalm 95. This psalm serves as both a <u>call</u> and <u>guide</u> to worship. True to form, as the people praised and worshipped, God spoke to them. Praise and worship go hand-in-hand. Remember, praise is the process of celebrating, glorifying, boasting about, and giving thanks for God and His wonderful deeds. Praise opens the door to worship; we must go through praise to get to worship. Worship is the act of surrendering to God, giving reverence, homage, and honor. Praise is about God, while worship is to or with God. When we move from praise to worship, we have transitioned into the presence of God and are communing with the Lord.

The psalmist begins by calling us to rejoice. As we enter the temple of God, we should come forth joyously. During praise, we "sing for joy" and "shout aloud" (vs. 1), lift up words and songs of thanksgiving, and make music (vs. 2). The psalmist not only provides us with instruction about the methods of praise, but He also provides the basis for our praise in verse 3-5. "For the Lord is the great God," "the mountain peaks belong to him," "the sea is his." Notice the psalmist's reasoning: 1) God is greater than all, and 2) God is the creator and possessor of all. Praise focuses on the enormity of God and the extent of His acts.

In verse 6, the writer transitions into worship. We are called to bow down before God. God has received the praises of His people and now He abides with His people. While praise includes a great deal of talking about God and talking at God, worship is the time to talk with God. Although this is a time of exchange, it is primarily a time for us to listen. The Hebrew word for worship most commonly used in the Old Testament means to prostrate oneself. We literally "get low" before God, laying down our wills, lives, and agendas in reverence of God and the superiority of His plans for us. It is here that we accept our lowly positions as the "people of his pasture, the flock under his care" (vs. 7) and acknowledge His superior position as our Lord.

"Call to me and I will answer you and tell you great and unsearchable things you do not know" (Jeremiah 33:3). God promises to respond to us as we worship. He faithfully responded to the worship of His people in Psalm 95:10-11. God spoke to the people of Israel assembled in the temple about the downfall of their ancestors. This may not have been what they wanted to hear, but it was what they needed to hear. "And my God will meet all your needs according to the riches of his glory in Christ Jesus" (Philippians 4:19). God will give you exactly what you need to travel down the path that He desires for you to go. "In their hearts humans plan their course, but the Lord establishes their steps" (Proverbs 16:9).

As you praise and worship God today, do so with a surrendered heart and a mind committed to obey. A bent knee is insufficient; God wants a tender heart. "Today, if you hear his voice, do not harden your hearts" (vs. 8).

Psalm 96

Your praise should be an evangelistic tool. As Christians, we are followers of Jesus Christ; we profess a commitment to live by His teachings. Before Jesus ascended, He commissioned His disciples: "All authority in heaven and on earth has been given to me. Therefore go and make disciples of all nations, baptizing them in the name of the Father and of the Son and of the Holy Spirit, and teaching them to obey everything I have commanded you. And surely I am with you always, to the very end of the age" (Matthew 28:18-20). The acceptance of this Great Commission, this call to evangelize, resulted in the birth of the Church. The witness of Jesus lived on because of the obedience of the 11 disciples. This same command has been given to us. As Christians, each of us has a responsibility to do our part to help evangelize the world.

The writer of Psalm 96 begins this text by calling the people to sing the praises of God to the nations. He is calling people to tell their testimony. Sing a new song. Sing your song. No one can tell your story like you. Your story needs to be heard because it is powerful. The story of who God has been to us, what He has done for us, where He has brought us from, and where He is promising to take us is one of the best evangelistic tools. Why? Because it is based in truth. It is not based on hearsay or opinion; it is a living witness of real life events and transformation. When we share our testimony with someone they can hear our love for God in our voices, see the gratitude on our faces, and experience the passion we possess for Christ in our body language. Our testimony--your testimony, brings the Gospel to life.

The writer calls us to "Declare his glory among the nations, his marvelous deeds among all peoples" (vs. 3.) Make a list of five things that God has done for you below. Wait. Write the big stuff; the stuff only God could do. If you could have done it for yourself or another human could have done it for you exclude it from the list.

1.

2.

3.

4.

5.

Now, think of a person who would be encouraged by hearing each of these things. Whose faith would be strengthened? Whose trust in God could be restored? These five items are the foundation of five testimonies. The people in your life are waiting to hear about "his marvelous deeds" (vs. 3) and "his salvation day after day" (vs. 2). I charge you to tell it! I implore you to tell it! Go and make disciples...the nations are waiting for YOU.

Psalm 97

Our God is King, so we can rejoice. This is our take away for today. Bad things are happening in your life. The world seems to be going to hell in a hand basket. Evil appears to be prevailing. Injustices occur daily. All of this may be true, however; our God is King so we can and should rejoice. The prevailing, eternal, and universal kingship of our God is good news, because this means that our God reigns above all. God is bigger than all people, places, and things. He reigns above all of your problems, concerns, and any reality that you can think of or experience. Our God is STILL on the throne. This is cause to rejoice.

I hear the thoughts rolling around in your head, "why should I rejoice when things are so upside down?" The answer is found in verses 10-11: "He guards the lives of his faithful ones and delivers them from the hand of the wicked. Light is shed upon the righteous and joy on the upright in heart." We win. You should rejoice because the Word of God promises that in the end, you win. If the Word promises it then the matter is settled. "So is my word that goes out from my mouth: It will not return to me empty, but will accomplish what I desire and achieve the purpose for which I sent it" (Isaiah 55:11). Say it aloud, "I win." If you faithfully hold on to God during the dark and hard times, God will guard your life until the day of victory (vs. 10). This does not mean that trouble will not come down your street, but that God will watch over you during those times. You will not walk through darkness alone and you will not face defeat. God will illuminate your path, so that you can see your way through. You win. Rejoice my sister. Rejoice my brother.

Not only do we win, but the adversaries of God also lose. Every force that sets itself up against God and His people will lose. In the end, we take a "W" and they take an "L." "Fire goes before him and consumes his foes on every side" (vs. 3). Just as the righteous have cause to rejoice in knowing they are covered by God's protection, His foes should be filled with terror. The clouds and thick darkness that surround God are warnings of His holiness, which His enemies cannot approach. God's holiness will also devour evil, as God "consumes his foes on every side" with fire. Evil, ungodliness, and unholiness cannot stand before our holy, righteous, and faithful God, nor can it defeat God's people.

Be encouraged today. Remember the words of Psalm 27:2-3 "When the wicked advance against me to devour me, it is my enemies and my foes who will stumble and fall. Though an army besiege me, my heart will not fear; though war break out against me, even then I will be confident." Why? Because you are covered by God's hand of protection, which shall guard you through times of adversity. You will see the victory. In the end, you win!

Psalm 98

Today, the psalmist calls each of us to demonstrative praise. Although there are many ways to give God praise that are reserved and covert, that is not what the psalmist is calling for in Psalm 98. He is commands us to glorify God in ways that are affectionate, emotional, open, overt, and expressive. Many would argue that there are times to offer God praise using constrained and internal methods, but today is not that day. This writer calls us to celebrate the Lord and His reign, with joy and expressions that can be seen and heard.

We are called to sing (vs. 1), shout (vs. 4), burst into jubilant song (vs. 4), play the harp (vs. 5), and blast the trumpet and ram's horn (vs. 6). A praise party is in order. With the same passion, excitement, and fervor that we celebrate our birthdays, weddings, anniversaries, and other accomplishments we are to praise the Lord. Many of us bring this type of joy to every party and celebration; it does not even have to be a special occasion. With little effort, we sing and dance to the Top 40 all night long. This psalm writer invites us to bring this same type of celebration into the temple and offer it to God as praise. If we are willing to sing and dance without reason, we should definitely be willing to offer our voices, our bodies, and the expressions thereof to God in thanksgiving and praise. The psalm writer offers a few reasons that we should offer jubilant praise: 1) He has done marvelous things (vs. 1); 2) He has made His salvation known (vs. 2); 3) He has revealed His righteousness to the nations (vs. 2); 4) He has been loving and faithful (vs. 3); and 5) He has saved people all around the world (vs. 3). What reasons do you have to offer God great praise?

All of creation is also called to offer demonstrative praise as well. The seas have been commanded to make sounds of praise (vs. 7). The rivers have been called to clap their hands and the mountains to join together in song (vs. 8). If these soulless objects of creation can demonstrate their thanksgiving and glorify the God of all creation, how much more can we as God's chosen people, royal priesthood, holy nation and special possession who have been called out of darkness into God's marvelous light give God praise (1 Peter 2:9)? Food for thought today.

Psalm 99

Today, we continue in the spirit of praise. The psalmist persists in His expressions of admiration and honor of God. He boasts of the magnitude of the character and name of the Lord. God is great and exalted (vs. 2), His name is great and awesome (vs. 3), and He is mighty and acts justly and rightly (vs. 4). How can we not praise a God like that? We serve a God who is second to none in character or deed. The writer points to an additional characteristic of God four times in the text; God is holy.

What does it mean that God is holy? God is distinct, separate, set apart, in a class by Himself. Holiness expresses the distance between God and creation. He is pure and we are impure. Humanity has been corrupted by sin and He is incorruptible. God is the reigning King of all creation and we are the created beings, serving at His mercy. God is eternal and we find eternal life only through Him. There are significant differences between who God is and the reality of who we are not. The Lord is King and "he sits enthroned between the cherubim"; the earth quakes in humble response as it recognizes its lowly position and God's supreme one. We too are called to respect and respond to this gaping distance known as holiness.

There are few appropriate responses to the holiness of God. The writer of Psalm 99 outlines a few of them. One of them is praise. "Let them praise your great and awesome name—he is holy" (vs. 3). Another is worship. "Exalt the Lord our God and worship at his footstool; he is holy" (vs. 5). Finally, there is obedience. "He spoke to them from the pillar of cloud; they kept his statutes and the decree he gave them" (vs. 7). When God tells us to do something obedient compliance with His command honors His holiness. Obedience is an act of submission, which recognizes the authority of the one giving the command.

Isaiah 6:3 says "And they were calling to one another: "Holy, holy, holy is the Lord Almighty; the whole earth is full of his glory." Recognize the holiness of God today. Offer Him praise. Spend time in worship. Obediently follow God's commands.

Psalm 100

Today, the psalmist continues providing insight about praise. This psalm is intended for giving thanks; it could have followed the collection of a thank offering in the temple in Jerusalem. While Psalm 98 taught us about demonstrative praise during corporate worship, this psalm instructs us on our posture as we enter the temple.

Verse 4 commands us to "enter his gates with thanksgiving and his courts with praise; give thanks to him and praise his name." Our praise and thanksgiving does not begin when we arrive at church nor does it commence when the organ is fired up and the worship leader stands before us. The psalmist says that we are to "enter" with thanksgiving and praise; we are to come through the doors already in this posture. This means that the shouts of joy and joyful songs called for in verse 1 must begin before you enter the church. We are not to enter the temple cold, but instead our spirits should already be warmed up during our personal time of praise.

Having worship leaders, choirs, bands, and dancers during corporate worship is important and biblical. "Your procession, God, has come into view, the procession of my God and King into the sanctuary. In front are the singers, after them the musicians; with them are the young women playing the timbrels" (Psalm 68:24-25). These leaders and their respective gifts edify the body of Christ, but each individual must be his/her own personal minister of worship. These temple leaders are not available to us at home, on our jobs, in our cars, or in our other places of daily visitation. As children of God and followers of Christ, we must possess the ability to praise God and offer thanksgiving for His wonderful deeds without the direction or guidance of others.

Our personal time of praise and thanksgiving prepares us for corporate worship. When we wake up Sunday morning honoring God with our prayers and songs of praise, our spirits are ready to join with others and go higher together. Corporate worship should be a continuation of our times of personal praise and worship, not a replacement or substitute. If we fail to do the prep work for corporate worship, our corporate experience will be stunted. We are not ready to go higher corporately because much of the body enters worship in a praise deficit. The worship leader has to prompt and prod the congregation. All the junk that we picked up throughout the week must be extracted to free us up to enter a place of corporate praise and worship. But if we have spent individual time before the Lord, God has already begun to lift the burdens of the week.

Think about it like a fuel tank. If you come to church on empty, then you must be filled all the way up for the corporate journey. You have nothing to give, because you are on "E." But if you come to church with your take ½ full, it will take less effort to fill you up. As a matter of fact, you can actually begin the journey because you have fuel inside of you. The fuel you receive during worship will simply add to what is already there. You have something to contribute to the corporate experience when you arrive. If you enter with a full tank, you are ready to go and keep going. You can pour out fully. Your praise is uninhibited by an empty tank or the junk from the week. You have something to offer to the corporate experience. Any fuel you receive during worship can simply be stored away for later in the journey.

My brothers and sisters, the posture that we enter the worship experience with is significant. I challenge you to prepare your heart and mind through personal praise and thanksgiving before entering the doors of the church. Offer God prayers, sing your favorite hymns, or create a play list with your favorite gospel songs so that you are ready for the corporate experience.

Psalm 101

How are you livin'? This is the question that this psalm of David forces us to ask ourselves today. How are you livin'? We read about King David's commitment to devote his personal and professional life to God. This devotion required him to "be careful to lead a blameless life" (vs. 2). David used the words "I will" nine times throughout the psalm to describe his conduct in an effort to glorify God.

Blameless does not mean sinless. If it did, David would have failed as soon as he made this promise. So would we. Blameless simply means possessing integrity. God calls us to live an undivided life by walking in wholehearted devotion to Him and His statues. God calls us to live godly at all times and not be chameleons — bending and flexing for circumstances and people. "Jesus Christ is the same yesterday and today and forever" (Hebrews 13:8). God challenges us to be like Jesus — consistent. Jesus had impeccable character and lived a life of integrity. His virtues were unchanging, His mission was firmly rooted, and His passions were unmovable. Since Jesus knew who He was and whose He was, Jesus was comfortable in His own skin. This is the first requirement for living a blameless life — you must know who you are and to whom you belong. Failure to know yourself and what God says about you allows you to conform to the opinions, beliefs, and behaviors of others. We must be steadfast and immovable when faced with the temptations of our flesh and others.

We must also know the Word of the Lord. What does God say about that circumstance? About that behavior? About that activity? Failure to know the Word of God will cause us to operate with a divided heart and mind. David said, "I will set before my eyes no vile thing" (vs. 3). I like to practice the "lead me not into temptation" principle. Meaning, I avoid people, places, and things that could lead me down a course of sinful behavior or that could weaken my resistance to evil. If you are trying to lose weight, that means avoiding the bakery section at the grocery store. If you are trying to save money, that means not going to your favorite store. Matthew 26:41 teaches us that the "flesh is weak"; so I place no confidence in mine. It sounds like David didn't either, because he did not allow vile things to even enter his sight.

Living a blameless life also requires us to break fellowship or avoid fellowship with certain people. Age-old wisdom teaches us "birds of a feather, flock together." We pick up behaviors, thought patterns, and ways of being from those with whom we associate. David recognized this and made a decision; "men of perverse heart shall be far from me; I will have nothing to do with evil" (vs. 4). We also need to run, not walk, from people that we do not want to be like. David committed that his "eyes will be on the faithful in the land, that they may dwell with me; he whose walk is blameless will minister to me" (vs. 6). Only those who were living the blameless, integrous, and undivided life that David wanted to live would advise him, speak into his life, or find a place in his inner circle. We should also pledge to surround ourselves with the faithful and blameless.

I have chosen a life of moral integrity, what will you chose today?

Psalm 102

Today, we read the prayer of a deeply afflicted man. He cries out to God for mercy in the midst of his distress. He begs for God to hear his prayer and respond with deliverance. In fact, his suffering is so severe that his bones burn, his heart withers, and he has lost his appetite (vs. 3-4). Unlike some of the other writers, his distress is not only the result of the conduct of his enemies, but his suffering originates from the wrath of God (vs. 10).

Despite his hardship, the writer is confident that God will have compassion and respond to his prayers (vs. 17). Not only is he assured that God will deliver him, but also that this deliverance will bless others. In verse 18 he writes, "let this be written for a future generation, that a people not yet created may praise the Lord." The psalmist understands that his life is not his own. That everything he is going through is for the glory of God and for the benefit of those yet to be born. His anguish, pain, and suffering are "so the name of the Lord will be declared in Zion and his praise in Jerusalem" (vs. 21).

The writer does not trust human memory or oral tradition to record this testimony, but instead calls for it to be written. His call for a written record was quite uncommon during the time that this prayer was prayed because history was passed from generation to generation orally in ancient Israel. This psalmist anticipated a time when history would be documented in writing and believed that his testimony needed to be heard.

What story do you need to record so that generations to come will be blessed? What testimony do you need to write down so that unborn readers might place their faith in God? I challenge you to "write down the revelation and make it plain on tablets so that a herald may run with it" (Habakkuk 2:2). You have truth to offer the future, but it must be recorded. Don't hesitate, start today.

Psalm 103

The psalmist resumes his instruction on praise today. After commanding his soul and his entire being (mind, body, and spirit) to praise the Lord in verses 1 and 2, the psalmist shares with us the benefits of praising God. Not only is God glorified and magnified by our praise, praise is beneficial for us as well. David lists seven spiritual benefits of praise: forgiveness, healing, redemption, love, compassion, satisfaction, and renewal.

The first benefit of praise is forgiveness of our sins. What incredible news! As humans, we are sinful creatures. Unfortunately, it is part of our nature. With God's help, we can do that which is right, but apart from God we are unable to resist sin's temptation. "For I know that good itself does not dwell in me, that is, in my sinful nature. For I have the desire to do what is good, but I cannot carry it out. For I do not do the good I want to do, but the evil I do not want to do—this I keep on doing. Now if I do what I do not want to do, it is no longer I who do it, but it is sin living in me that does it" (Romans 7:18-20). With sin having such a powerful grip on us that it causes us to fall short, even when we desire to walk in obedience, to receive forgiveness of sins in exchange for our praise is an act of God's grace. Thank the Lord for this benefit today.

The second benefit is healing. God is able to heal all our diseases, but He does not have to do so. Healing, like every other move of God, is subject to God's sovereignty. I am grateful that my praise inclines God's heart towards me and the infirmities of my body.

Satisfaction was among the benefits of praise mentioned by David. To experience fulfillment and contentment is truly a gift from God. The world cannot offer us satisfaction, no matter how hard it tries. The systems, institutions, and things of this world cannot fulfill us, and our flesh that craves the things of this world is never satisfied either. Ecclesiastes 1:8 says "all things are wearisome, more than one can say. The eye never has enough of seeing, nor the ear its fill of hearing." Only God can bring us the peace of mind, body, soul, and spirit that results in satisfaction. As we lift up praise to our God and King, He showers us with peace so that we experience satisfaction in Him and Him alone.

Renewal is another benefit of praise. I don't know about you, but I often find myself tired. There are seasons where I go to bed tired and I wake up tired. I am simply exhausted. But when I enter a state of praise and worship, I am renewed. I am refilled. I am replenished. In the presence of God, I forget how tired I was before I got there. I sing, dance, and shout before the Lord with the same fervor and energy of a professional athlete. My body is renewed as I lift up the name of Jesus. I also find renewal of mind in praise and worship. Remember, praise is all about focusing on God, who He is, and what He has done. The more I focus on God, the less I focus on me, my problems, and my prayer list. In praise, all my worries melt away. Try it. God promises to renew the youth of those who praise Him so that we may soar like eagles. Eagles fly to and fro effortlessly. As you praise God, He will allow you to move through life with ease and grace like an eagle flying through clear blue skies.

Praise the Lord, my brothers and sisters, "and forget not all his benefits" (vs. 2).

Psalm 104

Today, we read a hymn to God as creator. I don't know about you, but I walked away thinking "my God is a bad dude!" The writer takes the creation account found in Genesis 1 and uses it to paint an incredible image of creation being formed by Elohim (Mighty Creator). He also provides excellent imagery of what our King looks like as He reigns over the entire universe.

The writer begins by describing the clothing of our King. His clothing includes splendor, majesty, and light (vs. 1-2). What does that even look like? Other kings where fine linens, metals, and even jewels, but our God is wrapped in light and adorned with majesty and splendor. The word splendor is customarily used to refer to the condition of a person, place, or thing as splendid or wonderful. Similarly, majesty usually refers to one's sovereign power or reign or even the greatness of a person, place, or thing. Our God is not only splendid and majestic, but He wears splendor, majesty, and light. "God is light; in him there is no darkness at all" (1 John 1:5). Wow! Our God is so holy that even His clothing reflects His nature. That is a bad dude!

Next, the psalm writer describes God's commanding power over skies and nature. God stretches out the heavens (vs. 2), lays beams on the waters (vs. 3), rides in the clouds, and on the wind (vs. 3). Then He uses the wind and thunderbolts as His agents (vs. 4). Really God?! Our God is a bad dude! Who else has this kind of authority, strength, or power? Our God is not only above the clouds, the highest thing that our human eyes can perceive, but He rides in them. While we ride in cars, buses, trains, and even planes, Elohim rides in the clouds. While we are blown to and fro by the wind, God rides on it. While we take cover during thunderstorms, God uses the wind and thunderbolts to do His work. The very elements of the storms that we fear are at the mercy of God's greatness and sovereignty. Our God is big and mighty and powerful. "Lord, our Lord, how majestic is your name in all the earth! You have set your glory in the heavens" (Psalm 8:1). Is there anything for us to fear when we serve a God like Elohim? Besides, if God is with you, what can mere mortals do to you (Psalm 118:6)?

Place your trust in the Creator today; the one robed in splendor, majesty, and light. The one who rides in the clouds and commands the wind and thunderbolts. If God can do all of that, He can take care of little 'ol you today. Remember, your God is a bad dude!

Psalm 105

Today, we are reminded that God keeps His promises. Period. Say it with me, God keeps His promises. I believe it. I am confident of it. I know it for sure, because the Word of God says it. "Know therefore that the Lord your God is God; he is the faithful God, keeping his covenant of love to a thousand generations of those who love him and keep his commandments" (Deuteronomy 7:9). "Not one of all the Lord's good promises to the house of Israel failed; every one was fulfilled" (Joshua 21:45). "God is not human, that he should lie, not a human being, that he should change his mind. Does he speak and then not act? Does he promise and not fulfill?" (Numbers 23:19)

Psalm 105 takes us through a historical account of how God kept the covenant that He made to Abraham in Genesis 15:9-21. When Abraham was 75 years old, God promised to give his descendants the land of Canaan. He was childless at the time and his wife was well beyond childbearing years. Nothing about this promise made logical sense, but "Abraham believed the Lord, and he credited it to him as righteousness" (Genesis 15:6). Has God made a promise to you that seems absolutely outrageous? One where you can't help but think, no way? The writer of Psalm 105 provides sufficient rationale for why you should believe God. Take Him at His Word. He walks us through how God kept His promise to Abraham throughout the generations; even after he was dead and gone.

God not only protected Abraham, but He also kept their covenant from returning void. First, God gave him descendants, Isaac, Jacob, and then the people of Israel (vs. 9-10). Second, God allowed no one to oppress the people of Israel or to harm them (vs. 14-15). Third, God made provision for them to withstand famine (vs. 16-22). Fourth, God multiplied the people of Israel, even in the midst of hardship (vs. 24). Fifth, God made provision to bring them out of Egypt (vs. 26-36). Sixth, God brought them out of Egypt with great wealth and provision (v. 37). Seventh, God was with Israel as they traveled through the wilderness (vs. 39). Eighth, God supernaturally provided Israel's needs in the wilderness (vs. 40-41). Finally, God gave them the land of

Canaan (vs. 44). God watches over His Word/promises to ensure it is performed (Jeremiah 1:12).

As Christians, we are the people of God. The same care and concern that God gave to perform the promise made to Abraham, He will also give to protect the promises made to you. Place your trust in the Promise Keeper today. God has not forgotten you or the promises He made to you. Just as He remembered His covenant with Abraham and took 9 steps to perform it, He will remember the one He made with you.

Psalm 106

The human memory is an interesting, yet problematic thing. Far too many of us have inconsistent memories. We rarely recall events accurately, but instead only from our vantage point. Some memories are deleted from our minds all together, while values and beliefs are often conveniently forgotten. Lets face it; many of us are like two year olds with memories failing to extend beyond the length of our arms. We are easily distracted, redirected, and refocused on that new thing, new feeling, new desire, and the latest person, place, or thing that fits our current agenda. This was the M.O. (modus operandi) of the people of Israel.

The writer of Psalm 106 gives us a history lesson of the persistent forgetfulness and rebellion of the people of Israel despite God's continuous grace and mercy. God faithfully brought Israel out of Egypt and across the Red Sea (vs. 9-10), but they forgot His faithfulness and "did not wait for his counsel" but instead grumbled and complained about their inability to find water (Exodus 15:22-26). Then they built a golden calf and worshipped it at Horeb because "they forgot the God, who saved them, who had done great things in Egypt" (vs. 21). God continued to keep Israel safe in the wilderness, but "they yoked themselves to the Baal of Peor and ate sacrifices offered to lifeless gods" (vs. 28). This song and dance of God caring for Israel and Israel's forgetfulness is outlined again and again throughout Psalm 106. Israel could not seem to remember God and His wonderful deeds performed on their behalf.

What was wrong with Israel? The same thing that is often wrong with us; their memory was shorter than their need for God. We are all guilty of forgetting what God has previously done or who He has previously been to us. Assess the mental files of your past. What do you tend to forget? Do you find yourself worrying about your finances when God has not only promised to provide "all your needs according to the riches of his glory in Christ Jesus," but has repeatedly done so each and every time you were in a bind (Philippians 4:19)? Are you worried about that health issue when the Word declares that Jesus was "pierced for our transgressions, he was crushed for our iniquities; the

194

punishment that brought us peace was on him, and by his wounds we are healed" and He has healed you before (Isaiah 53:5)? What is it that you can't seem to remember?

Take your selective memory to God in prayer. Ask Him to bring back to your remembrance His promises and witness in the areas of your life that you seem to forget when the rubber meets the road. Make a decision to remember in the future. Israel's inability to remember cost them 40 years in the wilderness and a long stent in exile. What will your forgetfulness cost you?

Psalm 107

We have more to learn from the mistakes of ancient Israel. I'm sure you've heard the colloquialism "doing the same thing and expecting different results is called insanity." Today's psalm shows us how much this statement applied to the people of Israel. The writer spends forty-three verses telling us how Israel persisted in doing the same thing over and over again.

Israel had a persistent pattern of behavior. It began each time with Israel in some type of distress or hardship. They wandered in the desert, hungry and thirsty (vs. 4-5). Then they cried out to God for help (vs. 6). God graciously responded to their cries and delivered them from their hardship (vs. 6). God led them out of the wilderness into the promise land (vs. 7). Israel praised God for His faithfulness and deliverance (vs. 9). Then they rebelled against God. Although the rebellion is not expressly mentioned in this first example of the psalmist it was stated in the third and fourth stanza of the psalm. Each time that God graciously extended grace and mercy to Israel, they eventually rebelled again.

What was it that made Israel continuously repeat this pattern? Did they enjoy the darkness and the deepest gloom (vs. 10)? Probably not. No more than you or I enjoy the punishment and discipline that we experience when we rebel and disobey. Was it that Israel failed to truly love God? That is unlikely. I doubt that God's chosen people loved God any less than we do as the Body of Christ. Maybe they lacked a true desire to serve God. I doubt they were any less committed than we are today.

What caused Israel to create a pattern of rebellion, crying out to the Lord in distress, and seeking divine deliverance? The answer to this dilemma is found in the beginning. Genesis 2:7 "the Lord God formed the man from the dust of the ground"; Genesis 3:1 "now the serpent was more crafty than any of the wild animals the Lord God had made"; and Genesis 3:15 "and I will put enmity between you and the woman and between your offspring and hers." Although we were made in the image and likeness of God and we have the Spirit of God living in us, we were made from dust. That dust keeps us from being completely spiritual beings; it is what makes us human and not little gods. Then there is the issue of sin and the spiritual war at work between God and Satan that is played out in the hearts, minds, and actions of humanity. Just as our flesh, which often leads us away from the will of God is real, so is the sin that keeps us from living the lives we desire to live in God. "Although I want to do good, evil is right there with me" (Romans 7:21). The enemy and his schemes and attacks pull us away as well. "The thief comes only to steal and kill and destroy" (John 10:10).

There was good news for Israel and there is good news for us as well. The Lord had great love for Israel (vs. 43). He did not treat Israel as their sins deserved, but instead extended abundant grace and mercy to them. The same is true for you. God loves you and will rescue you, even when you sin against Him. "'Because he loves me,' says the Lord, 'I will rescue him; I will protect him, for he acknowledges my name'" (Psalm 91:14). Isn't it refreshing to know that you have the love of God on your side? If so, "give thanks to the Lord, for he is good!" (vs. 1)

Psalm 108

Today, we meet David again. He has written a psalm praising God for His great love and praying for protection against his enemies. What an interesting combination. On the one hand David sings "be exalted, O God, above the heavens, and let your glory be over all the earth" (vs. 5) and on the other, "save us and help us with your right hand" (vs. 6). Praise and petition are separated by only one verse-one breath. From the same mouth flows loving adoration and desperate need. "Yet for us there is but one God, the Father, from whom all things came and for whom we live; and there is but one Lord, Jesus Christ, through whom all things came and through whom we live" (1 Corinthians 8:6). David recognized that God was the sole object of his affection and the source of his strength.

The key nugget for us today is found in verse 12, "for the help of man is worthless." David knew that only God could safely deliver the people of Israel and grant them aid against their enemy (vs. 12). Who is your source? Who are you looking to solve your problem, handle your situation, and provide for your need? While it is nice to have the assistance of family, friends, and colleagues, God is ultimately the one who we really need. David knew the truth of Psalm 54:4, "Surely God is my help; the Lord is the one who sustains me." Do you recognize that anything a human being can do for you is only due to the enabling of God? "For it is God who works in you to will and to act in order to fulfill his good purpose" (Philippians 2:13). God enables human beings to act. Any favor that you have received from anyone is only because God touched that person's heart or enabled them to bless you. "Every good and perfect gift is from above, coming down from the Father of the heavenly lights" (James 1:17). If your Heavenly Father is the one holding the master plan of your life and the resources to meet your needs, why run to any one else?

I encourage you to place your trust in the one who will not disappoint you today. While trusting in humans to help you is worthless, trusting in God is always worth it. The one who trusts in God finds happiness. "Blessed is the one who trusts in the

Lord, who does not look to the proud, to those who turn aside to false gods" (Psalm 40:4).

Psalm 109

Today, David prayed for God to deliver him from false accusers. They attacked him without cause with their lying and hateful words (vs. 2-3). To add insult to injury, David's friends had turned to foes (vs. 4). Unfortunately, this was a familiar place for David and this is also a familiar place for many of us. A trusted advisor turns on you, becoming a Judas. A child grows greedy, becoming an Absalom. A boss or mentor develops jealous feelings, becoming a Saul. A lover takes your prized possessions, becoming a Delilah. Betrayal is devastating. It often hurts us to the core. This is where we meet David today, broken hearted as he cries out to God "for I am poor and need, and my heart is wounded within me" (vs. 22).

David pleads for justice. He asks the Lord to handle his accusers. He asks for them to lose their leadership positions (vs. 8), lives (vs. 9), wealth (vs. 10-11) and so much more. I get it; David is suffering and in the heat of the moment he wants them to suffer too. The anger, frustration, and distain that he is experiencing are only natural and are likely warranted. Our feelings are real and are a natural response to external stimuli. However, we can't stay there; allowing our feelings to drive us. Notice that David didn't stay there. Look at verse 4. "In return for my friendship they accuse me" he said "but I am a man of prayer." David prayed for his slanders. He prayed for his accusers. He prayed for his enemies, just as he prayed for his friends that forsook him in Psalm 35:13-14; "Yet when they were ill, I put on sackcloth and humbled myself with fasting. When my prayers returned to me unanswered, I went about mourning as though for my friend or brother. I bowed my head in grief as though weeping for my mother."

God knows that we will become disappointed, angry, and hurt when our enemies attack us, but He expects us to resist the temptation to sin. "'In your anger do not sin.' Do not let the sun go down while you are still angry" (Ephesians 4:26). God also expects us to pray for our enemies, despite the fact that they are harming us. "But I tell you, love your enemies and pray for those who persecute you, that you may be children of your Father in heaven" (Matthew 5:44-45). Prayer is an act of love. It may be hard, but we are called to extend this type of love to those who harm and hurt us. Besides, the Holy Spirit intercedes on our behalf not just when we are faithful and obedient children, but even when we mess up and don't know what to pray (Romans 8:26). We receive grace so that we can be gracious. We receive mercy so that we can be merciful. We are loved so that we can extend love.

Pray for your enemies today. Call them by name. Ask the Lord to bless them and keep them.

Psalm 110

Our brother David shows up again today to provide us with a Prophetic Psalm. He is prophesying about the reign of the coming messiah, who we now know as Jesus Christ. David foresees that this coming King would be a mighty warrior (vs. 3), eternal priest (vs. 4), and an anointed judge (vs. 6). All of His enemies would be defeated, becoming a footstool for His feet (vs. 1). David prophesied that Jesus would be a king like none other. None of the great kings of Israel possessed all of the attributes of Jesus. While David may have been a great and mighty warrior, he was not an eternal priest. Samuel, known for his wisdom, was a wise judge but he also was not an eternal priest. Only Jesus Christ is "a priest forever in the order of Melchizedek" (vs. 4); this is good news for us as His followers.

God gave the people of Israel the Levitical Priesthood through the bloodline of Aaron while wandering in the wilderness. Among other things, these individuals were responsible for teaching the tribes of Israel the law of the Lord, inspecting ceremonially unclean persons, and maintaining the tabernacle. The high priest served as an intercessor for the people of Israel. Only he could enter the presence of God. Only he could offer sacrifices for the atonement of their sins. Are you starting to see a problem here? This priesthood was imperfect. It was based on one's bloodline and regulations, not on an indestructible life. Romans 3:23 says "for all have sinned and fall short of the glory of God." These priests were sinners, just like the people for whom they interceded.

Our Savior, our High Priest, who sits at the right hand of God (vs. 1) did not come through the line of Aaron. His priesthood is similar to Melchizedek's (see Genesis 14:18). He was appointed directly by God, not on the basis of the law, regulation or his bloodline, but based on the sovereign will of God. Melchizedek was appointed based on the witness of His own life and not his family of origin; Melchizedek stood on his own witness. His priesthood was also forever. It was not limited to 25 years of service, like the Levitical Priesthood; Melchizedek died a priest and therefore his priesthood is superior to the Levitical Priesthood. However Jesus' priesthood surpasses them. Only

Jesus had an indestructible life. "Now there have been many of those priests, since death prevented them from continuing in office; but because Jesus lives forever, he has permanent priesthood. Therefore he is able to save completely those who come to God through him, he always lives to intercede for them" (Hebrews 7:23-25).

I hope you did not miss the good news in that Hebrews scripture. Since Jesus' priesthood is eternal we have someone interceding on our behalf FOREVER! Because He died for our sins, they are atoned for FOREVER! And because Jesus sits on the right hand of the Father speaking on our behalf, we can enter God's presence, boldly and confidently FOREVER (Hebrews 4:16, New King James Version)!

Praise God for your High Priest today!

Psalm 111

In today's psalm, we find another laundry list of reasons to praise the Lord. The writer reflects on the works, deeds, and redemption of God (vs. 2-9). The message is clear, our God is incredible and does awesome things for His people, hence is worthy of sincere and heartfelt praise (vs. 1) After calling forth praise, the writer drops a word of wisdom for us "the fear of the Lord is the beginning of wisdom; all who follow his precepts have good understanding. To him belongs eternal praise" (vs. 10).

As children, most of us feared our parents. If they said to get good grades in school, we worked to get good grades. If they gave us a curfew, we honored it with timely return home. If they ordered us to be quiet, we immediately ceased talking. Why? We were afraid of the consequences of noncompliance. For most people, failure to comply with the commands, rules, or will of our parents would result in discipline of some sort; we were afraid of our parents. Maybe you weren't, but I was afraid of mine. I am referring to a healthy fear. This fear was based in reverence, respect, and honor. Children should not be petrified, horrified, or terrified of their parents and we should not be of God. The Bible often uses the word "fear" to refer to reverence of God. Think of verse 10 this way, the reverence of the Lord is the beginning of wisdom (LDJ translation). Just as it was wise to reverence our parents, we have much to gain by reverencing God.

Fear of our parents led to obedience to them. The same should be true of our relationship with God. Out of love and respect for God we should "follow his precepts" (vs. 10); we should do what He says. It is just that simple. Our obedience is a reflection of our fear of God and our disobedience is an indication of a lack thereof. Like little children, we often test the limits. We make decisions contrary to the will God, just as we did without our parents. In many cases, we do so unconsciously. Usually, we find that these choices or actions were unwise through the consequences we face. The more we grow in our relationship with God the more we revere, honor, and fear Him, the more we submit to His will and Word concerning us. To reach the places that God has prepared for us, we must maintain a reverential fear of the Lord; this is the keep to obtaining spiritual wisdom and understanding.

Just as our fear of our parents kept us out of a lot of trouble, it also led us into a great deal of good. Remember the words of Jeremiah 29:11 "'For I know the plans I have for you,' declares the Lord, 'plans to prosper you and not to harm you, plans to give you hope and a future.'" If we want to step into the prosperous plans of God then obedience is required of us. I challenge you to allow the fear and reverence of the Lord to guide you today.

Psalm 112

The psalm writer continues his instruction on fearing the Lord from Psalm 111:10, where he declared, "the fear of the Lord is the beginning of wisdom." Today, we learn about the many benefits of fearing God, which are tied to our obedience. Remember, fear of God = respect and reverence of God = obedience to God, His commands, and His Word.

The psalmist identifies ten benefits of fearing the Lord:

1. **You are blessed.** When we obey God we are rewarded, God bestows His favor upon us, and we can enter a persistent state of happiness and prosperity.
2. **Your children and future descendants will be blessed.** The godly are not only personally rewarded for their reverence, but their bloodline reaps a harvest as well. Here, the writer identifies influence and positive reputation as two of the benefits received by our heirs.
3. **You will receive wealth and riches.** Psalm 32:8 says "I will instruct you and teach you in the way you should go; I will counsel you with my loving eye on you." God is willing to provide us with instruction and counsel on every aspect of our lives. There is also guidance in the Word of God concerning every area of our lives, including our finances and careers. Obedience to this instruction is key.
4. **You receive enduring righteousness.** When we reverence God, we seek to live lives that honor Him. The blue print for righteousness is found in the life of Jesus, as documented in the Word. When we humbly seek to live the life that Jesus lived, righteousness is not an occasional characteristic, but a persistent state of being.
5. **Good comes to you.** You will not have to seek out that which is good, but it will look for you. Good people, good jobs, good environments, and good opportunities will all seem to fall into your lap. All of these are rewards of fearing God. "Surely your goodness and love will follow me all the days of my life" (Psalm 23:6).
6. **You will never be shaken.** Bad things happen to good people; that is the way life works. However, the godly

will be able to stand in the midst of it all. Why? Because their foundation is solidly established by God and His Word. "No weapon formed against you shall prosper, and every tongue which rises against you in judgment, you shall condemn. This is the heritage of the servants of the Lord, and their righteousness is from me," says the Lord" (Isaiah 54:17). Weapons form, but they cannot prosper.

7. **You will be remembered forever.** The people of God have a beautiful legacy that lives on eternally.

8. **You will not fear bad news and will triumph over any foes.** There is nothing to fear when we trust in and obey God. Instead, our hearts are steadfast and calm. We are able to live and act with peace, knowing that "if you say, 'The Lord is my refuge,' and you make the Most High your dwelling, no harm will overtake you, no disaster will come near your tent" (Psalm 91:9-10).

9. **You will receive honor.** The Lord remembers those who fear Him. When we live lives that are pleasing to God, God will honor us and place us in positions to be honored by other humans as well.

Our God is gracious enough to reward His servants who revere Him. He does not have to bless us, but He chooses to do so. Give God the thank offering of your fearful obedience today.

Psalm 113

Today, the psalmist provides us with another nugget about praise. Verse 3 says, "from the rising of the sun to the place where it sets, the name of the Lord is to be praise." God deserves praise from the location of the sunrise to the place where it sets. The sun rises and sets all over the earth. People in Africa and Asia see the sunrise and sunset. People in North America and Antarctica experience the sunrise and sunset. All of creation witnesses the sunrise and the sunset and therefore all things and all people should praise God. There is something universal about the day beginning and the day ending according to the placement of the sun. Just as the sun is universally recognized and needed, so is our God. Our God is the God of all persons and all things. Similarly, God is universally due honor and praise. All of creation has been created to praise the Lord. The form of praise may vary by nation, tribe, ethnicity, culture, class, race, gender, talents, experience, and church, but God is to be praised by all. "The Lord is exalted over all the nations, his glory about the heavens" (vs. 4).

There are times during worship services when it seems that praise could go on all day. People sing, dance, run, shout, clap, wave their hands, and otherwise express adoration and thanksgiving to God. In response, many proclaim that "it doesn't take all that!!!" and "when is this going to end?!" The writer of Psalm 113 suggests that the spectators may be wrong and the praisers may just be on to something. The naysayers may have missed the universal call to praise God. Praise is not a spectator sport. All of creation has been created to lift up the name of Jesus. How long are we expected to praise God? Try praising Him until you run out of things to praise and thank God for. If you run out of reasons to say "thank you" and exhaust characteristics of God to boast about, then you can stop praising Him. Life, health, and strength—thank you! Food, clothing, and shelter—thank you! Healer, deliver, and way-maker—You are worthy! Friend, lover, and protector—Hallelujah! Gracious, loving, and kind—Glory! It seems to me that we could praise God from the time the sun rises until it goes down and continue until it rises again.

Hebrews 13:15 says "let us continually offer to God a sacrifice of praise--the fruit of lips that openly profess his name." Decide to offer God continuous praise today.

Psalm 114

Although the meaning of the scriptures are unchanging, we can find fresh revelation in them based on changing conditions – the who, what, when, where, why, and how of our lives. I'm sure you've read a passage for the hundredth time, but saw something new on the hundred and first time. Similarly, we can come to a passage and find ourselves reading it over and over and over wondering what we are supposed to extract. I encourage you to persist in reading and praying for revelation when that happens. Continue to read the passage repeatedly, even if it takes days, until God speaks to you. Among the many reasons we study the Bible is to receive guidance, encouragement, and revelation from God for our lives. Join our brother Jacob in saying, "I'm not letting you go 'til you bless me" (Genesis 32:26). This is what happened to me with Psalm 114; I got stuck. But I stayed here until God illuminated something for me and for you. It took a week of reading the text over and over again, but it was worth it!

Today, we have a brief recount of the exodus of the mighty people of Israel from Egypt. This psalm is not focused on the historical perspective of the event, but the impact the event had on creation. "The sea looked and fled, the Jordan turned back; the mountains skipped like rams, the hills like lambs" (vs. 3-4). The earth quaked, the skies thundered and sent forth lightning, the waves raged; the earth trembled! All of creation responded to the presence and move of God in this majestic event. God did not sheepishly bring Israel out of bondage, but did so conspicuously with vengeance and miraculous wonders. Remember, between Exodus 7 and 11 there were ten plagues brought down on Egypt. Blood was shed, life was lost, animals and insects filled the land, people were struck with illnesses, and the lights went out on the earth. All of creation experienced this forceful freeing of God's people from slavery.

God will go to the same lengths to free you from your bondage. The people of Israel were the chosen nation of God. You too are among God's chosen. "You are a chosen people, a royal priesthood, a holy nation, God's special possession, that you may declare the praises of him who called you out of darkness into his wonderful light. Once you were not a people, but now you are the people of God; once you had not received mercy, but now you have received mercy" (1 Peter 2:9-10). God desires for you to be free, not enslaved by anyone, anything, or even any ideology. God wants you to be free! Jesus came for you to be free! "It is for freedom that Christ has set us free. Stand firm, then, and do not let yourselves be burdened again by a yoke of slavery" (James 5:1). But if you find yourself bound up in sickness, unforgiveness, debt, unhealthy relationships, false doctrine or sin, our God will move heaven and earth to free you. "No temptation has overtaken you except what is common to mankind. And God is faithful; he will not let you be tempted beyond what you can bear. But when you are tempted, he will also provide a way out so that you can endure it" (1 Corinthians 10:13). Just as God parted the Red Sea to bring Israel out of Egypt, God has a plan to free you. Seek His will concerning you and obediently follow the plan He reveals to you. Then sit back and watch the earth and all of creation tremble in the presence of our mighty God as He moves to save and deliver you.

Psalm 115

Why do we get so scared, unsettled, and worried about what the ungodly have to say? Israel was constantly bent out of shape by the verbal attacks of their enemies. The book of Psalms is filled with petitions and cries for deliverance from the slander of neighboring countries. These nations neither knew nor served God. Instead, they worshipped idols made of gold, stone, and other materials. Although they were not subject to the covenant between God and Israel, lacked the protection of God that came with being His chosen people, and would not benefit from the promises of God, the people of Israel were constantly shaken by the taunts of these enemies. Why?

Whenever the people of Israel faced hardship, their enemies would ask, "Where is your God?" (vs. 2) Clearly, this was not an innocent question, but instead was filled with implications that the God of Israel had abandoned them, was powerless, or even non-existent. Instead of standing firm in the confidence of their covenant with God, the people of Israel would tremble with fear and often began to doubt God. The appropriate response to this question is found in verse 3 of Psalm 115, "our God is in heaven; he does whatever please him." Not only was the God of Israel alive and well and even present with the people of Israel, He was sovereign. God could move however, whenever, and wherever He desired--even allowing trials to descend upon His chosen people. Israel's enemies were limited in their ability to understand the God of Israel by their knowledge of their own gods. Their gods were not sovereign, but instead were man made-- created by humans using gold and silver (vs. 4).

Idols are lifeless and therefore powerless. "They have mouths, but cannot speak, eyes, but cannot see. They have ears, but cannot hear, noses, but cannot smell. They have hands, but cannot feel, feet, but cannot walk, nor can they utter a sound with their throats" (vs. 5-7). The gods of Israel's enemies were helpless. Therefore their taunts and attacks were meritless. Their idols could not help them or hurt them; they could not guide them or discipline them. The gods of Israel's enemies were simply a waste of the gold and silver from which they were made.

Not only are idols powerless, but so are the people who make and worship them. "Those who make them will be like them, and so will all who trust in them" (vs. 8). Just as idols have no mouths, eyes, ears, hands, feet, or voices neither do those who erect them or worship them. These people should be ignored. They are powerless. They are distractions. Israel's enemies had no business asking, "where is your God?" They were simply puffing, blowing smoke, and distracting Israel from trusting in the God of all creation. "The thief comes only to steal and kill and destroy" (John 10:10). Israel allowed their enemies to steal their peace and faith in God each time they chose to listen to their taunts. They also allowed them to jeopardize their relationship with God each time they chose to worship these idols, knowing that God forbade idol worship.

I challenge you to "submit yourselves, then, to God. Resist the devil, and he will flee from you" (James 4:7). Fix your eyes, ears, and hearts on God and God alone. Do not allow the idols of this world to distract you or unsettle you. Greed, materialism, competition, selfishness, self-reliance, and pride are among the modern day idols that we must resist. We must also silence the voices of those who have bought into their systems and who live by their rules. Do not allow them to speak over your life or to distract you from the life of abundant peace and joy that is found only in God.

Psalm 116

"The Lord is gracious and righteous; our God is full of compassion" (vs. 5). This verse is a summation of the characteristics of God seen by the psalm writer as he experienced God's saving power. In a time of great distress, the writer cried out to the Lord and God answered with deliverance. "For you, O Lord, have delivered my soul from death, my eyes from tears, my feet from stumbling" (vs. 8). The psalmist is filled with so much gratitude for the goodness of the Lord that he does not know how to respond.

Have you ever been here? So overcome with thanksgiving and awe for the gratitude, righteousness, or compassion of God that you did not know how to respond? Have you ever been rendered speechless by the way that God responded to your cry for mercy? Humbled by the saving acts of our God? I repeatedly find myself filled with so much emotion after God moves on my behalf that all I can do is weep. My knees grow weak under the weight of His glory and I fall prostrate to the floor. I am completely immobile in the face of God's grace and love towards me. Sound familiar? We are in good company. The psalm writer cried out in verse 12, "how can I repay the Lord for all his goodness to me?" Thankfully, he provides us with a few ways to respond to the goodness of the Lord.

First, we must accept the salvation of Jesus and allow Him to be the Lord of our lives (vs. 13). God wants our devotion. He desires that we humbly submit to Him and Him alone. God wants to be first in our lives; no person, place, or thing should come before God. "But seek first his kingdom and his righteousness, and all these things will be given to you as well" (Matthew 6:33).

Second, we must keep our promises to God no matter who is around (vs. 14). We often make vows to God in times of distress. We promise obedience. We promise righteousness. We promise to rid our lives of ungodly things and people. But after God brings us out of the trial into a place of triumph, we often fail to keep our promises. We must keep our vows to the Lord, no matter when they are made or who is around. God does not want fair weather followers, but unwavering devotion.

We find rest in God's grace, righteousness, and compassion, but we stay there through submission to His lordship. If you find yourself restless today, despite the goodness of God, command yourself to "be at rest once more, O my soul, for the Lord has been good to you" (vs. 7). Then check your devotion. Are you fulfilling the vows you made to the Lord? If not, self-correct and shift back into alignment.

Psalm 117

This is the shortest psalm in the Psalter; it is only two verses long. "Praise the Lord, all you nations; extol him, all you peoples. For great is his love toward us, and the faithfulness of the Lord endures forever. Praise the Lord." This is a call for universal praise. All people, everywhere, are called to lift up praise to God. The command is absolute. There are no carve-outs, caveats, or exceptions. The entire human race was created to praise God.

We often forget that Jesus did not die for a particular race or ethnicity, nation, or tribe. But He died for all persons, born and unborn. One man, for all of creation, paid the penalty for human sin. For this reason, we have been commanded to evangelize the entire world. Not simply those in our immediate sphere of influence, but those in other states, countries, and continents. Jesus left us with the Great Commission: "therefore go and make disciples of all nations, baptizing them in the name of the Father and of the Son and of the Holy Spirit, and teaching them to obey everything I have commanded you. And surely I am with you always, to the very end of the age" (Matthew 28:18-19).

Since we are called to take the Gospel to all nations, we must lay down our fears, prejudices, and ignorance concerning other races, tribes, and cultures. We must become open to learning, understanding, and accepting one another for our similarities and differences. God desires that all persons know and praise Him. We are meant to be instruments, used to effectuate His will in the earth. Ask God to purify your heart today, removing any barriers to effective disciple making across color, race, gender, class, and cultural lines. The King and kingdom depend on you.

Psalm 118

Today, we meet the psalm writer in another Hymn of Praise and Thanksgiving for deliverance from enemies. Although the subject matter seems redundant, it unfortunately is not; "the thief comes only to steal and kill and destroy" (John 10:10). The thief or enemy is persistent in his purpose. He continues to attack until he is successful in stealing, killing, and destroying. For that reason, we face one altercation after the other with the enemy of our souls. The same was true of Israel's enemies. As Israel exited Egypt, they traveled through one land after another, facing one group of enemies after another. Their enemies persisted in attacking them until they were either successful or until God moved on Israel's behalf or enabled them to overtake their enemies. As a result, dealing with enemies was a constant reality of the people of Israel.

Most of these psalms reflect the cry of God's people as they faced a new enemy, new battle, or new set of opposition. The same rings true for us. Even if we face the same opponent, each encounter feels like a new attack, battle, or set of resistance. We face fresh hurt, pain, discouragement, and distress--all requiring the help of God. As the psalmist reflects upon his latest hardship, he shares his learning with us; "it is better to take refuge in the Lord than to trust in man" (vs. 8). This statement is based in personal experience, not the testimony of another. Like many of us, the psalmist seems to have placed his trust in other humans in the past and received inadequate responses. How many times have you expected someone to love you, care for you, protect you, help you, or be there for you and they fell grossly short of meeting that need? Too many to count, right? The writer of Psalm 118 learned his lesson, "the Lord is with me; he is my helper" (vs. 7). He also learned that the love of humans is fickle, while God's "love endures forever" (vs. 1). We must learn to place our trust—confidence, faith, and reliance—in God and God alone. Not in the government. Not in our pastors or churches. Not in our jobs. Not in our relationships. But in God alone! "It is better to take refuge in the Lord than to trust in princes" (vs. 9)

Until you learn to take refuge in God alone, you will continuously find yourself heart broken, disappointed, and dejected. Our God is tried and true, while humans are led by their emotions, circumstances, and flesh. We are completing unreliable. "Trust in the Lord forever, for the Lord God is an everlasting rock" (Isaiah 26:4, English Standard Version). Rocks are strong, solid, and unchanging. Take refuge in the Rock of your salvation. God is able to keep you!

Psalm 119:1-24
Aleph, Beth, Gimel

A bit of background: Psalm 119 is a devotional Acrostic writing about the Word of God, with one stanza (subsection) for each letter of the Hebrew alphabet. Within each stanza, all of the verses (8 in total) begin with the corresponding Hebrew letter. With 176 verses, this is the longest psalm in the Psalter (book).

Although the writer of these first three stanzas teaches us a great deal about the Word of God, I'd like our focus to be on verses 10 and 11 today; "I seek you with all my heart; do not let me stray from your commands. I have hidden your word in my heart that I might not sin against you." While the Word of God should be instrumental in our lives and obedience to the laws, precepts, statutes, and commands of God comes with many blessing for us, our devotion should be to God. The scriptures have significance for us because they are the Word of God, not the other way around. It is God that we love, serve, and adore. It is God that we are in relationship with. It is Jesus who saved us and redeemed us through His life and not simply through His Word. It is true that the Word of God is powerful; "for the word of God is alive and active. Sharper than any double-edged sword, it penetrates even to dividing soul and spirit, joints and marrow; it judges the thoughts and attitudes of the heart" (Hebrews 4:12). The Word has power, purpose, and weight because of the one whose mouth it flowed from. Without God speaking these words, the scriptures would lack the ability to transform, to impact, to rearrange, to bind and loose, and to withstand all scrutiny throughout eternity. It is God and God alone that we are to seek.

It is out of respect, love, and reverence for God that we seek to know, understand, and obey His Word. The writer cries, "open my eyes that I may see wonderful things in your law" (vs. 18). He has a thirst to know and to grow in God and the things of God. The writer goes on to write about the significance of obedience as the psalm develops. Why? Re-read 11; "I have hidden your word in my heart that I might not sin against you." He understands that failure to obey the Word of God not only keeps him from receiving God's blessings (vs. 1-2), but also leads to shame (vs. 6), and even death (vs. 17). Disobedience leads to something far more dreadful---sin against God! Failure to keep God's commandments is sinful and the writer did not want to experience this type of separation from God. Knowing, understanding, and following God's law was the way that the writer avoided sin.

"How can a young man keep his ways pure? By living according to the word" (vs. 9). The Word helps us to understand the character of the God we serve. From reading and studying the Word, we learn more and more about how God thinks, moves, and acts. We also receive guidance on how to live a life that is pleasing to God from the Word; for this reason the writer of Psalm 119:1-24 hid the Word in his heart. The heart is our center, from which every thought and action originates. "Above all else, guard your heart, for everything you do flows from it" (Proverbs 4:23). The writer committed to place the Word of God at the center of his being, thereby placing it at the center of his life. Everything flows from our hearts. Where have you placed the Word in your life? Where have you placed the God who spoke the Word in your heart?

I encourage you to hide the Word in your heart, so that you may live a life of obedience to God and His Word. Obedience to God's Word results in a blameless life and a blameless life results in receipt of God's blessings (vs. 1-2).

Psalm 119:25-48
Daleth, He, Waw

Today, the writer of Psalm 119 continues writing about the Word of God. In the Daleth stanza, he indignantly declares that he will obey the Word in both good times and bad. In the He section, he prays for instruction to flow from the scriptures. He concludes with the promise to share the Word with others in the Waw section. This psalm writer possessed a genuine love and appreciation for God's Word, which led to a sincere commitment to obedience.

Woven in between the dominant themes of these stanzas is a subtheme that can help us today; as we keep God's commands, His commands will keep us. The writer shares numerous ways that the Word can aid us and bless us, if we only trust and obey it.

First, the Word can strengthen us when our souls are weary (vs. 28); it has reviving power! When we are worn out, tired, and ready to quit, the Word reminds us to wait, hope, and trust in God; "those who hope in the Lord will renew their strength. They will soar on wings like eagles; they will run and not grow weary, they will walk and not be faint" (Isaiah 40:31).

Second, God's law keeps us from deceitful ways (vs. 29). The Word is able to guide us away from conduct that seems right, but leads to death, destruction, and sin. "There is a way that seems right to a man, but in the end it leads to death" (Proverbs 14:12). By teaching us the ways of God, the Word helps us to discern when a course of action is outside of God's will.

Third, God's precepts help us to avoid shame (vs. 31). Following God's commands helps us to avoid making mistakes that could result in humiliation, but instead lead us into blessings and deliverance from the tricks of the enemy.

Fourth, when we seek guidance from God's statutes our hearts are set free (vs. 32). Obedience to God and His Word brings us peace and joy. There is nothing to be anxious about when you know that you are following God's will. The Word is our guidebook for life and living God's way. Each time we read it and choose to obey it, we should rest in the confidence that God is pleased with our actions.

The writer provides many other ways that we are sustained when we obey God's Word: We avoid selfish gain (vs. 36), worthless things (vs. 37), and we are rid of disgrace (vs. 39). My favorite is that we find freedom (vs. 45) through obedience to the Word of God; "I will walk about in freedom, for I have sought out your precepts." As we seek to know, understand, and follow the Word of God we are not only delivered from the selfishness of our flesh, but from the bondage that comes from following the ways of the enemy and the world. The Word of God guides us into spacious places--unconfined by oppression, suffering, depression, mocking, and hardship. "It is for freedom that Christ has set us free. Stand firm, then, and do not let yourselves be burdened again by a yoke of slavery" (Galatians 5:1). The Word of God is the Rock on which we stand! Choose to remain free by submitting to its commands today.

Psalm 119:49-72
Zayin, Heth, Teth

Today, we learn of another benefit of knowing God's law — it gives us a leg to stand on. Our world is primarily governed by opinion and feelings. The candidate supported by the dominant beliefs wins the election. News is reported from the perspective of those individuals who financially control the airways. Individuals are convicted or freed based on the consciences of their peers. If you possess the minority opinion or are located on the fringes of society you are powerless in the face of opposition, suffering, need, or a desire to progress. You don't have a leg to stand on.

Fortunately, God and His systems do not function like the world. While human opinions and feelings are constantly changing, God is consistent, steady, and reliable. While a change in public or expert opinion can impact the price of fuel, the numbers on the NASDAQ, and the decision to go to war, it has no impact on the character of God. "God is not human, that he should lie, not a human being, that he should change his mind. Does he speak and then not act? Does he promise and not fulfill?" (Numbers 23:19) The writer of Psalm 119 understood the character of God and significance of the Word — God does not change and neither does His mind or His Word.

Obedience to the Word of God gives us standing before God. One must have standing to bring a lawsuit in a court of law. He or she must be able to demonstrate that they possess the right to participate in the case based on harm experienced or some nexus between the law and their personal situation. When we read, know, understand, and obey the Word, we are able to say to God "remember your word to your servant" (vs. 49). Only when we know the law of God can we petition God concerning it. When we pray the Word we are speaking God's words back to Him; reminding Him of what He promised and planned.

Think back to your childhood and the promises your parents made to you. "If you clean up your room then I will take you to get some ice cream." "If you get all A's and B's then I will buy you the video game you desire." "If the house is clean when I come home then I will allow you to attend that pool party." After keeping your end of the bargain you had no problem reminding your parents of what they said. "Momma, you said!!!" "Daddy, you said!!!" It wasn't that they had forgotten, but you believed them when they spoke those words to you. Your parents were not promise-breakers! Neither is God. God promises us in Isaiah 55:11 that His Word "will not return to me empty, but will accomplish what I desire and achieve the purpose for which I sent it." Praying the Word of God is a call for God to remember. It is a demonstration of our faithfulness to study and obey God's Word and a request for God to show His faithfulness to us.

Just as a child can run to their parent and proclaim, "you said," we can pray to our Heavenly Father, "do good to your servant according to your word, O Lord" (vs. 65). Obedience to the Word gives us standing before God; we have a dog in the hunt. We have a right to ask God to remember His promises because we have kept ours. If God failed to keep His promises to us we would be greatly harmed—our faith would waiver, and our hope would be diminished. I implore you to study the Word, know the Word, understand the Word and the OBEY the Word so that you can go boldly before the throne of grace asking God to remember His promises to you.

Psalm 119:73-96
Yodh, Kaph, Lamedh

Today, the writer teaches us that the Word helps us to keep things in proper perspective. Romans 12:2 provides us with this challenge: "Do not conform to the pattern of this world, but be transformed by the renewing of your mind. Then you will be able to test and approve what God's will is--his good, pleasing and perfect will." Although we live in this world we are called to operate by a different set of rules—according to the Word of God. As we previously discussed, the world has its own playbook where greed, competition, selfishness, materialism, lust, hatred and a myriad of other evils are normative. Although we live in this world, we are not citizens; "our citizenship is in heaven" (Philippians 3:20). We must resist the temptation to drink the Kool-Aid by accepting the ways of this world as normative for our lives.

The Word reminds us of the rules that govern our lives. By revealing God's will, we are able to recognize wrong as wrong, evil as evil, ungodly as ungodly and sin as sin when we see it and encounter it. The Kaph stanza is filled with cries to God for help from affliction. The writer is being persecuted and is suffering greatly, but he recognizes the errors of his persecutors. Since the writer knew the Word, he understood how he should be treated. The persecution he experienced was contrary to the Word and therefore professed "the arrogant dig pitfalls for me, contrary to your law" (vs. 85). He also knew God's promise to deliver him in the face of persecution.

The world teaches us that we are the sole masters of our fate. We are in control of our destinies and lives. As a result, the good we experience is a result of the good we've done and the bad is created by us as well. Not so in the kingdom; God is in control and His Word governs all things. "Your word, O Lord, is eternal; it stands firm in the heavens. Your faithfulness continues through all generations; you established the earth, and it endures. Your laws endure to this day, for all things serve you" (vs. 89-91). Only God and His Word are trustworthy and will endure the test of time. As we study and understand God's Word, we are reminded of His sovereignty and our limits. The ability of humans to control their lives is a fallacy. This false doctrine blinds us, but as we read God's Word the blinders are removed helping us to see that "the earth is the Lord's, and everything in it, the world, and all who live in it" (Psalm 24:1).

It is imperative that as kingdom citizens we operate by kingdom rules and possess a kingdom perspective. It is easy to become deceived by the ways of this world. Only by remembering God's precepts will our lives be preserved (vs. 93). Ask God to help you see things as He does today.

Psalm 119:97-120
Mem, Nun, Samekh

Today, the writer teaches us that academic study of the Word is insufficient. We must put the contents of the Bible to practice in our daily lives. In so doing, we move beyond head knowledge of the Word to heart knowledge. Heart knowledge of God's precepts makes us wiser than our enemies (vs. 98), gives us more insight than our worldly teachers (vs. 99), and allows us to have more understanding than people twice our age (vs. 100). The writer teaches us how to make the transition from academic study to life study of the Word.

First, we must love the law and meditate on it (vs. 97). When we are in love, we think about that individual constantly. Even when we are trying to focus on other things, that person's face or words skip through our minds. Our love for that individual extends to our thoughts and actions. The same must be true of our relationship with God and His Word. When we meditate, we reflect on or contemplate something. Loving the Lord requires us to ponder His Word and to allow its truths to penetrate our hearts. Our minds and hearts must become filled with the Word of God so that we can be reminded of God's commands and precepts as we walk through each day. What is in you will come out of you.

Second, we must obey the Word (vs. 100-101). We have talked about obedience to God's commands over the past couple of days. Quite simply, obedience is about doing what God says. If He says do it, then we do it. If He says avoid it, then we avoid it. If God says go right, we go right. We don't attempt to negotiate our own rules or look for loopholes around His, we follow the way provided by the Lord.

Third, we must take pleasure in Gods precepts (vs. 103). Honey is among the sweetest foods created by nature. It brings flavor to coffee, tea, and desserts. God has provided it for our enjoyment and pleasure. The psalmist professed that God's laws are even sweeter than honey. The Word of God has been provided to help us grow and develop. It has also been given so that we may know more about God, His character, and His plans. This should be sweet, desirable, and enjoyable to us as His children. Just as a child hangs on His parent's every word, the Word of God should enamor us as well. We should feed on it and enjoy the pleasant taste of its truth.

God wants our devotion. He wants us to follow Him in loving obedience not out of obligation or compulsion. To do so, we must move from head knowledge to heart knowledge of His Word. Learn to love the Word of God, because it is filled with the nutrients you need to grow into the person that God created you to be.

Psalm 119:121-144
Ayin, Pe, Tsadhe

Today, the writer teaches us about the importance of understanding the Word of God. Reading, studying, and meditating on the Word is extremely important, but a lack of understanding can be problematic. Having knowledge of the scriptures without understanding them is like memorizing a mathematical or scientific formula, but lacking the ability to apply it. Although many of us know that $e=mc^2$ is the Theory of Relativity, we do not have a clue what to do with it. Such knowledge requires the wisdom of one knowledgeable in the sciences. The same rings true of the Word of God. The scriptures are filled with commands, precepts, laws, and guidance spoken by the wisest being that has ever or will ever exist. At the same time, there is much room for human misinterpretation, confusion, and misunderstanding of the Word. Job reminds of this fact in Job 11:7; "Can you fathom the mysteries of God? Can you probe the limits of the Almighty?" Without the help of the Holy Spirit we lack any ability to properly discern or apply the Word of God to our lives or circumstances.

The writer of Psalm 119 understood the complexity of the Word and his helplessness to understand it without God. He repeatedly prayed for understanding and discernment. "I am your servant; give me discernment that I may understand your statutes" (vs. 125). Far to often, our heart to serve God does not properly align with our understanding of the will of God. A servant is a person in service to another; one who is there to be of use by his master. How can we do the Father's will if we don't understand it? Serving God requires an understanding of His will and His Word. Without it, we can aimlessly run around acting on God's behalf doing things that do not please Him or that He doesn't desire for us to do.

Many different forms of writing are used throughout the Bible. Some texts are written allegorically, while others are packed with simile and other books are filled with poetry. In many cases, the meaning of the words on the page is not found in the literal construction of the text. We need understanding and discernment to interpret the Word of God. Discernment allows us to distinguish what we read. I encourage you to ask God what His scriptures mean as you read them, then ask God how He desires you to respond to His Word. "'My thoughts are nothing like your thoughts,' says the Lord. 'And my ways are far beyond anything you could imagine'" (Isaiah 55:8, New Living Translation). Responding to the Word of God requires us to humbly accept that we do not know or understand everything.

The writer also recognized that misapplication of the Word could lead to harmful consequences. He prayed, "Your statutes are forever right; give me understanding that I may live" (vs. 144). It is only when we clearly understand the plans of God, outlined in the Word, that we can properly follow them. It is like having directions to a friend's home. Only when they are clear and you understand them can you properly follow them and arrive at your destination without incident. If you don't understand the symbols on the map you can make a left turn when you should go right. If you can't interpret your friend's shorthand you are incapable of making proper traffic decisions. God's Word is like those directions. You need the mind of Christ and discernment of the Holy Spirit to follow them into the light and away from darkness. The writer declared in verse 105, "Your word is a lamp to my feet and a light for my path." Without understanding we still stumble through the darkness.

Pray and ask the Lord to grant you understanding and discernment before you start reading His Word.

Psalm 119:145-160
Qoph and Resh

The writer provides a bit of support for his faith and trust in the Word of God. In verse 151, he says, "yet you are near, O Lord, and all your commands are true" and in verse 160, "all your words are true; all your righteous laws are eternal." Our God is true and so is His Word.

The Hebrew word used for "true" in these stanzas is 'emeth which means stability, certainty, trustworthiness, assured, faithful, and right. Say it with me: The Word of God is stable. The Word is certain. The Word is trustworthy. The Word is sure. The Word is faithful. The Word is right. Choose to believe it. Stand on it. It is so.

Our world is constantly changing. The standard for beauty changes several times each decade. Laws are constantly amended, repealed, or overturned. The income level of the middle class drops regularly. The empowered political party changes at least once every 8-12 years. The "best schools" for our children is a moving target, as are the "good" neighborhoods. So much of life in the world is fleeting, but the Word of God is unchanging. What is the difference? The world's systems were created and are maintained by humans while the Word was spoken from the mouth of God--the God of stability, faithfulness, trustworthiness, and certainty. "It will not return to me empty, but will accomplish what I desire and achieve the purpose for which I sent it" (Isaiah 55:11). When a word is released from God's mouth it is destined for success—hitting the chosen target EVERY time. Because of this, we can stand on the Word with confidence and full assurance. The Word is true!

I challenge you to increase your faith in God by increasing your trust in His Word. God's Word is eternal. God's Word is true. Not because it has been recorded in a book called the Bible, but because of the one who spoke these words. No other words are as reliable, significant, or long lasting as the Word of God. The sayings of the wise can be forgotten. Mathematical and scientific formulas can be disproven. Laws can be challenged by culture and then repealed. But the Word is true and lasts forever.

Psalm 119:161-176
Sin and Shin, Taw

The Word of God should ultimately bring us peace. "Great peace have they who love your law, and nothing can make them stumble" (vs. 165). The Hebrew word used for "peace" in this text is shalom which means safe, well, happy, welfare, health, and prosperity. Those who love the Word of God are afforded the blessing of shalom.

In the Word, we find guidance, direction, and correction. We also learn about the character of God, the plans of God, and even the movement of God. The Word also gives us examples of people and their interactions with God at various points in human history. Finally, the Word helps us to understand the will of God for all creation. As a result, we come to understand God, the things of God, and ourselves better as we study. Studying the Word is a life long journey. As long as we have breath in our bodies there is more to know, understand, and apply to our lives. While on this journey we may experience moments of great joy on one extreme and conviction on the other. But at the end of day, we should experience shalom — the peace of God.

As Jesus prepared His disciples for His departure, He promised that the Holy Spirit would be sent to them. The realization that Jesus would not always walk among them caused many of them great distress, but Jesus blessed them with peace. "Peace I leave with you; my peace I give you. I do not give to you as the world gives. Do not let your hearts be troubled and do not be afraid" (John 14:27). The Word provides us with that type of peace; a peace quite different from that of the world. Worldly peace is based on circumstances and situations. If an individual has the right job, house, spouse, kids, financial stature, health situation, etc. then they can live in peace. But the Word teaches us that even during a storm we can live with the peace of God. In the midst of tragedy we can maintain peace; "the peace of God, which transcends all understanding, will guard your hearts and your minds in Christ Jesus" (Philippians 4:7).

The Word points us to the giver of peace and towards the path of becoming the children that God created us to be. There is safety, wellness, happiness, welfare, health, and prosperity in the will of God—which we find through His Word. Allow God to transform your life by becoming a lover of His Word; "Turn from evil and do good; seek peace and pursue it" (Psalm 34:14).

Psalm 120

"I call on the Lord in my distress, and he answers me. Save me, Lord, from lying lips and from deceitful tongues" (vs. 1-2). The writer, like many of us, has been lied on and is deeply disturbed. He desperately runs to God seeking help.

Why do lies bother us so much? People tell untruths and half-truths about us all the time. They lie about our character and our conduct. They even lie about our thoughts and intentions--as if they could really know them. Sometimes lies are told unintentionally or negligently and still others are boldfaced, big ugly, whoppers. Despite the type of lie, the nature of the lie, or the intention of the liar, the result is still the same—we get bent out of shape. Spend some time in prayer today asking God why you get so upset, bothered, or annoyed when people lie on you. Psalm 139:1-3 says, "You have searched me, Lord, and you know me. You know when I sit and when I rise; you perceive my thoughts from afar. You discern my going out and my lying down; you are familiar with all my ways." This means that God knows you and He knows the truth about you. You also know the truth about you and your actions, thoughts, and motivations, so... Why do lies bother you so much? John 8:32 says "You will know the truth, and the truth will set you free." Choose to walk in the freedom of your OWN truth today.

Notice the response that the writer of Psalm 120 anticipated; "what will he do to you, and what more besides, O deceitful tongue? He will punish you with a warrior's sharp arrows, with burning coals of the broom bush" (vs. 3-4). The liar will be destroyed. Although the lies may have been harmful and hurtful to the writer, the response of God is worse. God will respond with sharp arrows and burning coals. Ouch! The arrows of God's truth and the coals of His judgment are far more piercing than any lie that can be told on us.

Remember the call of the writer of Psalm 115 to trust in God and His truth; forget what people say, because it is unreliable anyway. "All you Israelites trust in the Lord—he is their help and shield. House of Aaron, trust in the Lord—he is their help and shield. You who fear him, trust in the Lord—he is their help and shield" (Psalm 115:9-11).

Psalm 121

Today, the psalmist teaches us about the character of God. Unlike many of the other psalms, we do not read a cry for help or a plea for mercy, nor do we read about the psalmist's enemies or foes, but instead we spend all eight verses reading about the nature of God. The psalmist did not stop with describing the wonderful attributes of God; he went on to explain how God's character blesses us. As I read these few verses, I could not help but to proclaim "what a mighty God we serve!"

1. **God is your help** (vs. 2). As the maker and creator of all things, God is in control of all things. "Nothing is impossible with God" (Luke 1:37, New Living Translation). God can move in the midst of any situation because He is the creator of all things.

2. **God is faithful** (vs. 3). The psalm writer says, "He will not let your foot slip." As you climb the mountains of life, you will not stumble or fall. No matter how treacherous, difficult, or dangerous the circumstances of life may become, you will win. Why? Because God does not sleep on the job. He is always watching over you and protecting you; "He who watches over you will not slumber" (vs. 3). For this reason, you can rest in the assurance of Romans 8:37 "in all these things we are more than conquerors through him who loved us."

3. **God is your protection** (vs. 5-6). Just as shade protects you from the sun and the moon lights your path at night, God will guard you from every threatening force. You have to trust God to look after you. "If you say, 'The Lord is my refuge,' and you make the Most High your dwelling, no harm will overtake you, no disaster will come near your tent" (Psalm 91:9-10).

Our God is a protector who "will keep you from all harm—he will watch over your life" (vs. 7). Notice that the psalmist said ALL harm. Not some harm. Not certain situations. But God will take care of *everything* concerning you, if you allow Him to do so. Decide to lift up your eyes to the hills today, for that is where your help comes from (vs. 1).

Psalm 122

Today, we meet David again in a Song of Ascents as he sings joyfully about Jerusalem. The psalmist rejoices at the conclusion of his pilgrimage to the great city. If the people wanted to encounter God during David's day, they had to press their way to Jerusalem. He had finally made it to the house of God and his heart was filled with joy.

Unlike you and I, the people of Israel had to travel significant distances to worship the Lord in the one place where God dwelled—Jerusalem. Some scholars believe this journey took weeks and even months, but it was the only way that they could worship God in His temple. You can imagine the affection that the Israelites had for this city; this was the city of their God and therefore the center of their lives.

The writer called the people to "Pray for the peace of Jerusalem: 'May those who love you be secure. May there be peace within your walls and security within your citadels'" (vs. 6-7). This call was for both internal and external peace, security, and prosperity. The sacristy of the city of God could not only be compromised by the attack of Israel's enemies, but also by strife among the people of Israel and financial hardship.

What the city of Jerusalem was to the people of Israel, the church is to Christians today. This is the place where we gather to worship God together. Fortunately, it is not the only place that we can meet God, hear from God, and praise/worship God, but it is the place where we can join with other Christians in doing so. Thanks to the presence of God living within us, God is everywhere that we go and He hears us each and every time we call out to Him. God desires that His children persist in assembling to worship and praise Him and our churches are the place where this occurs (Hebrews 10:25).

Pray for the peace of your church today! Pray for the security of your church today! Pray for the prosperity and effectiveness of your church today!

Pray with me: *God, we thank you for the Church universal today—the Body of Christ. We thank you that through it you touch and reach this dark and lost world. Thank you for each local assembly that gathers in your name, to preach and teach the Gospel, evangelize, worship, disciple and impact the lives of your people. I intercede on behalf of my church [insert church name], asking you to touch it, move in it, and through it so that you will be glorified. I pray for the peace of my church; peace within its walls and outside its doors. I thank you for prosperity in word, mission, deed, and motive. Bless it for the uplifting of your kingdom and the manifestation of your heart through the love it shows through its members. God, let my church be a place where you dwell always and where any man, woman, boy, or girl can come to meet you, know you, and love you. In Jesus name, Amen.*

Psalm 123

Today, we meet the writer in a low place. He cries out for mercy in the face of ridicule from arrogant and proud men. The writer recognizes that only God can help him and hence expresses total dependence on God to change his circumstances. Although this psalm is only four verses long, the writer professes twice that he will look to God and God alone for help.

Where are you looking for assistance? "The eye is the lamp of the body. If your eyes are healthy, your whole body will be full of light. But if your eyes are unhealthy, your whole body will be full of darkness. If then the light within you is darkness, how great is that darkness!" (Matthew 6:22-23) Where are your eyes fixed? Our eyes guide us to the destination on which they are focused, just as a lamp directs us through darkness to the place it illuminates. If your eyes are focused west then your feet will walk westward. If your eyes are fixed on a stop sign, then your car will head towards it. Likewise, if our eyes are fixed on God then our attention, thoughts, plans, and conduct will reach out to Him.

Fixing our eyes on God and God alone, places Him at the center of our lives. We are totally dependent on Him for wisdom, guidance, provision, and deliverance. Unfortunately, we tend to rely heavily on other people, circumstances, and institutions instead of depending on God. Psalm 146:3 says, "Do not put your trust in princes, in human beings, who cannot save." The New Living Translation says "Don't put your confidence in powerful people; there is no help for you there. It is better to take refuge in the Lord than to trust in humans." Human beings are flawed, selfish, inconsiderate, and forgetful; only God is faithful enough for us to depend on. God is faithful.

Endeavor to place your hope and trust in God today. Fix your eyes upon God and God alone; He will not disappoint you, because He is reliable and trustworthy.

Psalm 124

David is testifying today. He is giving God praise not only for delivering him, but also for delivering all of Israel. David knows that the people would have perished if the Lord had not been on their side. Israel would have fallen in the face of enemy attack (vs. 2), been consumed by their enemies' anger (vs. 3), and been overtaken by the flood and raging waters (vs. 4-5). God showed Himself to be a deliverer!

You can hear the relief in the writer's voice while reading this psalm. The people of Israel were in a bad situation and God seemed to step in right in the nick of time. "We have escaped like a bird out of the fowler's snare; the snare has been broken, and we have escaped" (vs. 7). Israel was almost a goner, but God snatched them out of the hands of their enemy. This is good news for us! God will deliver us; even when it seems that our enemies are about to overtake us.

At some point in our walk with God, we will also develop a Psalm 124 testimony; a situation when we can say "if the Lord had not been on my side, then..." Be it a car accident that should have killed us or a sickness that should have overtaken us or an enemy attack that should have destroyed our reputation. Maybe you went through a financial situation that should have ruined you or had a heartbreak that should have never healed. God has delivered each of us from something. If God has yet to deliver you, I encourage you to keep living. Your turn has not come yet, but it will come. Trials are inevitable (John 16:33); it will rain on every street at some point in time.

The great thing about encountering situations like the one reflected in this psalm is that they help us to draw closer to God and to learn more about Him and His character. Israel came to know that "our help is in the name of the Lord, the maker of heaven and earth" (vs. 8). We often hear that experience is the greatest teacher because we experience God best during our trials. What have your trials taught you about God? What do you know about God's character that you wouldn't have known without the test on the other side of your Psalm 124 testimony? Give God praise today for being that kind of God to you!

Psalm 125

Today, the psalm writer provides us with three benefits of trusting in the Lord:

1. **We cannot be shaken**
2. **We are surrounded by the Lord**
3. **The wicked will not rule forever**

Oh, what good news! If we rely on God, taking Him at His word, we will not be shaken (vs.1). Each day, we face opportunities for our faith to waiver--the balance of our bank account is less than our monthly bills; we begin yet another month unemployed; happily-ever-after was so long ago that we wonder if that healthy marriage was a memory or a dream; our prodigal son has yet to return home, despite our best efforts. You name it, life happens every day; pulling at the fibers of our relationship with God. Despite the persistent harsh realities of life, God's people will remain unmovable if we persist in trusting God. "As it is written: 'For your sake we face death all day long; we are considered as sheep to be slaughtered.' No, in all these things we are more than conquerors through him who loved us" (Romans 8:36-37). The fight has already been fixed, we win, BUT we must continue to trust in God to bring us through the fight successfully.

God is with us. "As the mountains surround Jerusalem, so the Lord surrounds his people both now and forevermore" (vs. 2). Cities protected by mountains are difficult to penetrate. The mountains serve as barriers blocking external forces from entry. Anyone attempting to enter the city must go over and through the mountains; neither of which is an easy task. The same is true for those who place their trust in God. When we trust Him, God will be the sustainable and unmovable force in our lives. Your enemy must go through God or around God to get to you, both of which are impossible! God is the defender of those who place their trust in them.

"The scepter of the wicked will not remain over the land allotted to the righteous" (vs. 3). God will preserve His people. Even when the wicked seem to succeed, it is only temporary. When we remain unwavering, God will persist in rescuing us. "Because of the increase of wickedness, the love of most will grow cold, but the one who stands firm to the end will be saved" (Matthew 24:12-13). God is the God of all. He is in control of all. He is the ruler of all and He will deliver His people from the hands of evil.

Be encouraged today. No matter what it looks like, trusting God is always the best option. God will not forsake you—despite how bad it looks. "Trust in him at all times, you people; pour out your hearts to him, for God is our refuge" (Psalm 62:8).

Psalm 126

Today, the psalmist shares a song of joy for the restoration of Zion. The people of Israel had returned home from Babylonian exile. Although their disobedience led the people of Israel into captivity, God's faithfulness had brought them out. Our God is a redeemer and restorer, even when we get ourselves in trouble.

The exile was a low point in Israel's history. They were removed from their land and taken into enemy territory. God's people were no longer free, but were the subjects of their enemies. As you can imagine, this period was characterized by sorrow, hardship, pain, oppression, and longing. When God freed His people, they came forth with laughter and songs of joy. "He who goes out weeping, carrying seed to sow, will return with songs of joy carrying sheaves with him" (vs. 6). God replaced every tear with smiles, laughter, and joy as the people of Israel were restored.

Restoration means to bring back, reinstate, or return to a former condition or position. God promised to restore the people of Israel to their pre-exile days in Isaiah 54. But Israel had to go through the exile to experience God's restoration. Although the exile was painful, their sin led them there. God had warned them and begged them to turn from their wickedness many times, but they would not relent, so God had to discipline them. Discipline leads to growth. When Israel learned the lessons that God needed to teach them, they were restored.

"'The Lord disciplines those he loves, and he punishes everyone he accepts as a son.' Endure hardship as discipline; God is treating you as sons. For what son is not disciplined by his father? If you are not disciplined (and everyone undergoes discipline), then you are illegitimate children and not true sons. Moreover, we have all had human fathers who disciplined us and we respected them for it. How much more should we submit to the Father of our spirits and live! Our fathers disciplined us for a little while as they thought best; but God disciplines us for our good, that we may share in His holiness. No discipline seems pleasant at the time, but painful. Later on, however, it produces a harvest of righteousness and peace for those who have been trained by it" (Hebrews 12:6-11).

Discipline is often necessary for us to mature and fulfill the destiny that God has planned for us. Are you in a season of discipline today? If so, be encouraged. You are going through this process for your good; for the good of your destiny. God loves you. If He did not love you, He would allow you to continue down the path of destruction. Just as your mother disciplined you to keep you from touching the hot stove and your father disciplined you to keep you out of the street, our Heavenly Father disciplines you to keep you away from enemy territory, fleshly desires, and other wickedness that could destroy your future. Submit to the discipline of God and trust Him to restore you after you've passed the test! This time is hard, but it is necessary it!

Psalm 127

Today, the psalm writer reminds us that it is God's blessings and not our human efforts that yield results in our lives. We are incapable of handling even basic things without the Lord's help.

He speaks first about our daily work; "Unless the Lord builds the house, its builders labor in vain" (vs. 1). Although most individuals spend roughly 40-50 hours a week working jobs to pay their bills, save for rainy days, and otherwise financially supporting themselves, all of this effort is fruitless without God. We NEED the God factor! God is our sustainer. It is He that blesses the work of our hands, allowing us to be productive, effective, and fruitful. "But remember the Lord your God, for it is he who gives you the ability to produce wealth, and so confirms his covenant, which he swore to your ancestors, as it is today" (Deuteronomy 8:18). "In their hearts humans plan their course, but the Lord establishes their steps" (Proverbs 16:9). If you find yourself unproductive or struggling with a task, seek the Lord. Ask God to work through you so that you do not labor in vain. Remember, you can do all things through Christ that gives you strength (Philippians 4:13).

Next, the writer speaks of our security; "Unless the Lord watches over the city, the watchmen stand guard in vain (vs. 1). All the security systems in the world cannot protect our homes from invasion, without the covering of the Lord. No army can protect our nation from terrorist attacks, we need God's guardian angels to look after us. God is our protection. "The Lord is my light and my salvation—whom shall I fear? The Lord is the stronghold of my life—of whom shall I be afraid?" (Psalm 27:1)

Finally, he speaks of the constant human attempt to meet or daily needs (i.e. food, clothing, and shelter); "in vain you rise early and stay up late, toiling for food to eat—for he grants to those he loves" (vs. 2). We will lie, kick, steal and scream to feed, clothe, and house ourselves. We will work long hours, stand in long government lines, and even seek benevolence from churches and agencies to ensure that we do not hunger, thirst, or sleep on the streets for too long. All of these efforts are fruitless without God, because God is our true provider. "And my God will meet all your needs according to the riches of his glory in Christ Jesus" (Philippians 4:19).

Ask God to help you keep things in perspective today. God is your sustainer, security, and provider.

Psalm 128

Today, we learn additional benefits of godliness. Specifically, the writer teaches us about the blessedness or happiness experienced by those who fear the Lord and obey His commands. Hence, our first take away is that reverence and obedience are forms of godliness.

Being a Christian means to be a follower of Jesus Christ and following Him means seeking to live the type of life Jesus lived and obeying the commands He gave us. Ephesians 5:1-2 says "follow God's example, therefore, as dearly loved children and walk in the way of love, just as Christ loved us and gave himself up for us as a fragrant offering and sacrifice to God." We live lives that are pleasing to God when we follow the loving example that Jesus provided for us. Jesus demonstrated His love for us and for God as He faithfully obeyed God, fulfilled His life's purpose, and loved His neighbor as Himself. We are called to do the same.

Our godliness is not without reward. The writer of Psalm 128 says that those who revere and obey God will eat the fruit of their labor and be prosperous (vs. 2). The work of our hands will be fruitful. Jeremiah 29:11 says, "'for I know the plans I have for you,' declares the Lord, 'plans to prosper you and not to harm you, plans to give you hope and a future.'" If we obediently follow the plans that God has for us, we will be led into prosperity, hope, and a future. That sounds quite simple, but unfortunately, we often deviate from the plan of God. We have our own ideas about what is best, the steps we should take or the direction we should go. However, if we remain obedient to Him and His Word then He will provide for our every need by making the work of our hands prosperous.

The godly are also promised fruitfulness in marriage. "Your wife will be a fruitful vine within your house; your songs will be like olive shoots around your table" (vs. 3). This verse not only refers to reproduction, but also faithfulness and sexual pleasure. Matthew 6:33 teaches us to "seek first his kingdom and his righteousness, and all these things will be given to you as well." If we take care of the things concerning God, He will take care of that which concerns us. The godly man or woman will be rewarded with a faithful spouse, healthy children, and great intimacy with their spouse; some call that the American Dream. ☺

The hymn writer says it this way, "trust and obey, for there is no other way, to be happy in Jesus but to trust and obey." Ask God to help you to trust and obey Him today.

Psalm 129

The writer of Psalm 129 lamented about the perpetual oppression of the people of Israel. With countless enemies encroaching upon them and a history of enslavement, the people of Israel were constantly in need of God's protection. Just as God chose Israel to be His people, its neighbors chose Israel to be their enemy. Israel's enemies constantly sought to enslave them or destroy their people and conqueror their land. It seemed that Israel had been dealt a bad hand.

Although every human being has bad days and experiences hard times, trials, and pain some people go through long seasons of hardship. It seems to be raining only on their side of the street, day in and day out. People look at these people and say—"wow, they have a hard life." Have you ever felt that way? Like your life was one bad day after the next?

The poor, orphans, homeless, and minorities are among those that seem to be living the hard-knock life. It appears that the cards have been stacked against them. Very few people advocate to protect their interests, they are constantly criticized, and few desire to help them rise above their situations. They live in persistent oppression, just as the people of Israel did.

This was not the end of Israel's story, although they faced constant threats of enemy attacks. The writer of Psalm 129 provides those going through hard seasons, facing persistent oppression, and living on the fringes of society with good news. "They have greatly oppressed me from my youth—let Israel say—they have greatly oppressed me from my youth, but they have not gained the victory over me" (vs. 1-2). Israel's enemies did not win. They did not gain the victory. They did not succeed in their attempts to permanently enslave them or eradicate them. Israel survived the attacks and oppression of their enemies. Yes, Israel went through hell and high water, but they survived it too! How? They had God on their side. "But the Lord is righteous; he has cut me free from the cords of the wicked" (vs. 4). God redeemed them.

If you are going through a hard season, be encouraged. God will not leave you there (Deuteronomy 31:6). Trouble won't always. Your enemies won't overtake you. Your circums. won't destroy you. You have God on your side. Be strong and courageous (Joshua 1:9). Hold on. Keep the faith. In the end, you will win!

Psalm 130

The psalmist calls us to do something that is counterintuitive today, run to God when we mess up. We have the propensity to run and hide when we make mistakes like toddlers being potty trained. Have you noticed that tots hide in the corner when they fail to timely respond to their urge to go to the bathroom? Why? Because it is at that point that they realize that they did something wrong and are afraid of the consequences. We, as adults, do the same thing to our Heavenly Father. Instead of running to God, we run away from God (e.g. Genesis 3).

The psalm writer teaches us to take a different approach to our sin. We should cry out to God when we mess us, not hide from Him. "Out of the depths I cry to you, Lord; Lord, hear my voice. Let your ears be attentive to my cry for mercy" (vs. 1-2). I know that you may be embarrassed, remorseful, saddened, or even guilt-ridden because of your sin, but don't allow those feelings to keep you from pursuing God. Allow these emotions to spark change in your mind and heart towards your behavior. Allow them to lead you to say the same thing as God about that action (wrong is wrong and right is right). Allow them to drive you towards a different course of future behavior. Next time, make a godly choice instead of a sinful one. There is no need to beat yourself up, because God doesn't plan to denounce you. "There is now no condemnation for those who are in Christ Jesus, because through Christ Jesus the law of the Spirit who gives life has set you free from the law of sin and death. For what the law was powerless to do, God did by sending his own Son in the likeness of sinful flesh to be a sin offering. And so he condemned sin in the flesh, in order that the righteous requirement of the law might be fully met in us, who do not live according to the flesh but according to the Spirit" (Romans 8:1-4). God does not condemn you; He forgives you (vs. 4).

Although God graciously sent Jesus to die for our past, present, and future sins we must still cry out to God when we mess up. God calls us to act as mature persons in our relationship with Him, which means we must take personal responsibility for our conduct; we have to fess up. "If we confess our sins, he is faithful and just and will forgive us our sins and purify us from all unrighteousness" (1 John 1:9). God is more than willing to help us out of the mess that we've gotten ourselves into, but we must be prepared to answer the age-old question "what did you do?" God is not condemning you when He questions your conduct; He is maturing you. He is helping you to take personal responsibility for your behavior, which frees you to make a different choice the next time that you are faced with the opportunity to fall into the same sin.

I am thankful that we serve a forgiving God, one who we can call out to when we mess up. God keeps no record of our sins (vs. 3), nor does He condemn us. Instead, He redeems us by His love.

Psalm 131

The psalmist pushes us to take another step toward spiritual maturity today. He challenges us to let go. "I do not concern myself with great matters or things too wonderful for me" (vs. 1). We often get caught up worrying about things that are above our pay grade. Should the janitor concern himself with what phone system the company uses? Should the pastor concern herself with the brand of sealant used to fix a crack in the floor? Should an infant care about the grade of gas his father purchases? Should a child worry about the kind of bread she eats? The answer to all of these questions is generally, no. These issues are outside of the scope of that individual's responsibility, expertise, or ability to comprehend and therefore they should not be of their concern. It is a fruitless exercise for any of these individuals to worry about these matters—someone else has these things covered.

We are often guilty of worrying about things that are above our pay grade. Most often, we get caught up worrying about tomorrow, but we don't control the future. God holds the plan for our lives. "Your eyes saw my unformed body; all the days ordained for me were written in your book before one of them came to be" (Psalm 139:16). Instead of trusting in the plan of God, we walk around concerned about the future of our careers, finances, families, health, and a plethora of other things. Where does your concern lead you? Have you been able to successfully control your future? No, right?! Because your future is above your pay grade; this is a matter too wonderful for you. God holds your future. Learn to let go of all attempts to control your future through worry or concern.

The writer of Psalm 130 provides us with guidance about how to begin to let go. We must relax and trust God. Verse 2 says, "but I have stilled and quieted my soul; like a weaned child with its mother, like a weaned child is my soul within me." When a child is being breastfed, they are totally dependent upon their mother's breast for sustenance, security, and comfort. Any time a breastfed child experiences any type of lack they cry until they are placed back on their mother's breast. As a child is weaned, it must learn to trust their mother to provide food, security, and comfort in ways other than giving him her breast. A bottle becomes an acceptable substitute for food and a pacifier provides comfort. Eventually, the child no longer expects the breast, but knows their needs will be met in some other form or fashion.

We must develop childlike faith in God. We must quiet our souls and let go of our concern for the future. We must learn to trust God to provide everything we need; just like a weaned child. We must come to know that God has made provision for our sustenance, security, and comfort. Read Matthew 6:25-34.

My brother, my sister, "put your hope in the Lord both now and forevermore" (vs. 3).

Psalm 132

It is easy to mistakenly label this psalm as a history lesson and then skip over it. Although this passage retells points in Israel's history, there is a nugget for us here. This psalm begins with a promise that David made to the Lord; "I will not enter my house or go to my bed, I will allow no sleep to my eyes or slumber to my eyelids, till I find a place for the Lord, a dwelling for the Mighty One of Jacob" (vs. 3-5). Later in the psalm, the promise that God made to David is recorded. "One of your own descendants I will place on your throne. If your sons keep my covenant and the statutes I teach them, then their sons will sit on your throne for ever and ever" (vs. 11-12).

David made a promise to God and God in turn made a promise to David. The particulars of the promises are not important for our purposes today, but this psalm shows us the mutuality of David's relationship with God. It is easy to end up in a one-sided relationship with God; a relationship where we walk around with a laundry list of expectations of God, making constant demands on Him, and engaging in lectures instead of conversations. Too often, God becomes our genie in a bottle instead of our friend, parent, or lover. God and David were in a relationship of mutual love, respect, and affection. David could rely on God and God could rely on David. The mutuality of their relationship was not based on David's perfection. He messed up, sinned, and fell short, but he always came back to this place of mutuality where he sought to please God, do His will, and give God honor and glory. David kept his promise to God and God kept His promise to David. Perhaps this is why David was called a man after God's heart, despite his obvious flaws and shortcomings.

Are you in a one-sided relationship with God? Can God count on you or can you only count on God? Can God ask something of you or can you only ask God for what you need and want? Are you listening when God talks or are you the only one talking?

Do some soul searching about your relationship with God. Where do you need to step it up? Commit to doing your part today.

Psalm 133

God desires for us to live in unity. It is good. It is pleasant. It is precious. It is blessed. Period. There are many things that separate people, just as they divided the nation that David inherited at the beginning of his kingship. But God's heart is set on harmony. This call to unity applies to individual believers and churches today, just as it did thousands of years of ago when God spoke this psalm through David.

Families, friends, churches, and denominations fight, but God desires peace. We are all children of God and need to learn to walk together in love. As Christians, we experience spiritual oneness in Christ (Galatians 3:26-29 and Ephesians 4:1-6) and therefore we must learn to flow as one. U-N-I-TY, you and I tie, bind, join together; this is God's heart. Remember the Great Commandments handed down by Jesus; "'Love the Lord your God with all your heart and with all your soul and with all your mind and with all your strength.' The second is this: 'Love your neighbor as yourself.' There is no commandment greater than these" (Mark 12:30-31). Our ability to live, remain, dwell together in unity is a reflection of our love for God and one another. It is the responsibility of each believer to maintain spiritual unity with his or her brothers and sister (see Ephesians 4:1-6). The key to doing so is found in verse 2 of Ephesians 4; "Be completely humble and gentle; be patient, bearing with one another in love." We must operate in humility, gentleness, and patience. The fruit of these acts of love is unity.

God is on a mission to draw all creation back to Himself. He wants every man, woman, boy, and girl to be saved. He is using the Church and believers to do this work in the earth. Disaccord, division, and dissention tear at the foundations of the Body of Christ. All of these things undercut the plans of God. A house divided cannot stand (Mark 3:23-25). I charge you with the words of Romans 12:18 today, "if it is possible, as far as it depends on you, live at peace with everyone." Ask God to help you to walk in unity. God blesses the unity of His children; He kisses it with His favor and holiness.

Psalm 134

Our psalm today is only three verses long, but there is still a word from the Lord for us here. In this simple call to praise and worship, we find a message for those who serve in the house of the Lord.

During Old Testament times, members of the tribe of Levi (the Levites) were responsible for ministry in the tabernacle and temple of God. When the people of Israel asked Aaron to erect a golden calf, while Moses worshipped on the mountaintop, the tribe of Levi repented of their actions and clung to the Lord. In response, God set them apart from the rest of the tribes to be His ministers among the people of Israel. Initially, they carried the Ark of the Covenant, ministered to and interceded on behalf of the people, cared for the tabernacle and its sacred furniture, and sang songs of praise and worship. King David added additional ministries such as the doorkeepers and treasurers.

This tribe's entire purpose was to do the work of the Lord; this was a 24/7 responsibility. "They were also to stand every morning to thank and praise the Lord. They were to do the same in the evening and whenever burnt offerings were presented to the Lord on the Sabbaths and New Moon festivals and at appointed feasts. They were to serve before the Lord regularly in the proper number and in the way prescribed for them" (1 Chronicles 23:30-31). Notice that they led worship EVERY morning and EVERY evening. They also served on high holy days AND regularly in the temple; doing the work that was assigned to them. Additionally, a prescribed number of them were required to serve in each ministry. The Levites were always on post, doing the work that God called them to do.

The writer of Psalm 134 was likely a ministry leader, calling the people to service. "Praise the Lord, all you servants of the Lord who minister by night in the house of the Lord" (vs.1). I am sure that serving in the tabernacle and temple day in and day out must have become burdensome for each individual at some point. The work of ministry is rewarding, but it can also be taxing. People singing in the choir, dancing, preaching, pastoring and serving as elders/deacons are constantly pouring out and ministering to other people—just as the Levites did for the other tribes of Israel. It seems that the writer of Psalm 134 recognized that his people needed to be refreshed. He cried out, "lift up your hands in the sanctuary and praise the Lord" (vs. 2). When we lift up praise to God, He responds by saturating us with His presence. This worship leader reminded the tribe of Levi to enter into personal praise and worship before trying to lead others. Those involved in ministry must work to maintain a healthy relationship with God in order to avoid burnout and to be refreshed. Praise is the key.

As you serve the Lord and His people, do not forget to take time to praise, worship, and pray. Allow God to refresh you, so that you can continue to pour out to His people.

Psalm 135

Today, the psalm writer provides us with more instruction on methods of praising God. He teaches us to use the Word as the substance of our praise. The writer reaches back to other places in the Word for inspiration and strings these verses together to create a great collaborative praise; every verse of this psalm is found elsewhere in scripture. Verse 1, "Praise the Lord. Praise the name of the Lord; praise him, you servants of the Lord" is recorded in Psalm 113:1. Verse 3, "Praise the Lord, for the Lord is good" can be found in Psalm 147:1. The writer continues quoting scripture for twenty-one beautiful verses.

There are numerous benefits to using the Word as the substance of our praise. Sometimes we can't find the right words to express our feelings; our hearts get so full of emotion that we are rendered speechless. This is a good time to turn to the Word for inspiration, particularly the book of Psalms. This book of the Bible covers every situation imaginable, written without pretense by the people of God. There are many times when I've turned to a psalm in an effort to find a way to express my feelings and found that the writer had perfectly captured my sentiment. As we read the Word of God, we discover that we are not alone—there is biblical witness to what we are going through and feeling.

The Word expands our view of God. One of the reasons that God gave us the Word was in order to know more about His character. Everything the Word says about God is true. You may have come to your time of Bible study only being able to express that "God is good" but after reading Psalm 135 you learn that the "Lord will vindicate his people and have compassion on his servants" (vs. 14). Serving a God that vindicates His people and who is compassionate provides you with two additional reasons to lift up the name of Jesus. Particularly in times that you find yourself in need of vindication and compassion. You are able to walk away from the Word with an expanded praise; "God is good because He will vindicate me and show me compassion!"

When you speak the Word, as your praise, you are agreeing with God about what He says about Himself. "All scripture is God-breathed and is useful for teaching, rebuking, correcting and training in righteousness" (2 Timothy 3:16). Every Word of scripture came from God's mouth. When we speak the Word to God, about God, we are reminding God of who He said He is and calling upon Him to manifest Himself in that way in our lives. When we speak God's Word, we express faith and reliance upon God to show up in our lives in the ways He promised. God does not forget what He promised, but He is pleased by our trust and confidence in Him and His Word.

Try using the Word of God as the substance of your praise today. It will propel you and your praise to another level.

Psalm 136

Today's psalm is full of good news. Actually it may be the best news I've ever heard, "His love endures forever." God's love is far-reaching and long lasting. So much so, it continues forever. The psalmist goes on and on in this psalm about the love of the Lord and the ways that God has expressed it to the people of Israel. His love brought them out of bondage, across the Red Sea, and into the promise land. Yes, Israel was not a perfect people, but God's love persisted despite their flaws, mistakes, and sins. His love endures forever.

The same is true for us. Because we are in Christ, nothing can separate us from the love of God; His love endures forever. Oh, what good news! Romans 8:38-39 says "for I am convinced that neither death nor life, neither angels nor demons, neither the present nor the future, nor any powers, neither height nor depth, nor anything else in all creation, will be able to separate us from the love of God that is in Christ Jesus our Lord." This means that nothing we say, nothing we do, and nothing we think can keep God from loving us. It also means that there is nowhere we go or NO-thing that we deal with that can keep us from God either!

The enemy may have tricked you into believing that the mistake you made or the sin you committed has caused God to stop loving you. The devil is a liar! Really, I mean it; the Bible says it. "He was a murderer from the beginning, not holding to the truth, for there is no truth in him. When he lies, he speaks his native language, for he is a liar and the father of lies" (John 8:44). He has deceived you. God still loves you and will always love you. Fortunately, God is not like man and has not and will not change His mind about you. His love endures forever.

Give God praise for His enduring love. It withstands our faults, failures, and shortcomings. It reaches us at our lowest points and extends up to the peaks of life as well.

Psalm 137

Today, we meet the psalmist in the midst of a lament about Israel's Babylonian exile. This was a difficult and painful time in Israel's history. Their king was dethroned, their land was destroyed, (including the temple), they were ejected from their land, their possessions were taken, and they were in bondage once again. Israel was hurt, humiliated, and helpless. So they wept. They lamented. They cried out to God.

As if exile was not bad enough, the Babylonians mocked Israel. "For there our captors asked us for songs, our tormentors demanded songs of joy; they said, "Sing us one of the songs of Zion!" (vs. 3) How rude?! How cruel?! These people had destroyed everything the people of Israel valued, stripped them of their promise land, and carried them off to a foreign land and then had the nerve to ask them to sing about it. This request was like pouring salt in an open wound; the Babylonians asked Israel to entertain them in the midst of their pain. It actually gets worse. The Israelites were not asked to sing just any songs, but the songs of Zion. These were the songs of praise and worship. These were the songs of the temple, which the Babylonians had destroyed. These were the songs devoted to God and God alone. Their captors expected to be praised!

The enemy of our souls is no different from the Babylonians. He appears to steal, kill, and destroy; tearing our lives, our relationships, and our faith to shreds (John 10:10). Leading us down the path of destruction, far away from everything that we value and hold dear. Then he torments us, whispering lies into our ears when we find ourselves at the depths of his pit. Finally, he demands to be praised. "Sing me one of the songs of Zion" Israel enemy commands. The devil desires to receive the glory and honor of God. Period. Look back over Matthew 4:1-11, when Satan attempted to trick Jesus into worshipping him. After commanding Jesus to turn a stone into bread and attempting to take Jesus' life, he asked Jesus to worship him. "Again, the devil took him to a very high mountain and showed him all the kingdoms of the world and their splendor. 'All this I will give you,' he said, 'if you will bow down and worship me.' Jesus said to him, 'Away from me, Satan! For it is written: 'Worship the Lord your God, and serve him only.'"

God alone is worthy of our praise and worship. The people of Israel knew this and became righteously indignant when the Babylonians expected to be praised. "How can we sing the songs of the Lord while in a foreign land?" they responded (vs. 4). This response was not simply an expression of sadness due to separation from Jerusalem, but an expression of the inappropriateness of their captor's request. Jerusalem was the City of God; the place where He dwelled and made His name great. It was the city to which all the people of Israel traveled to worship God. Although in captivity, the people of Israel refused to forget their vow to have no other god before the Lord (Exodus 20:3). They declared "may my tongue cling to the roof of my mouth if I do not remember you, if I do not consider Jerusalem my highest joy" (vs. 6).

Commit to remembering God today. Resist the taunts, torments, and tricks of the enemy. God is still on throne. Pray for increased discernment so that you can recognize the schemes of the enemy.

Psalm 138

Our God is big and mighty and great and powerful. He created all things, knows all things, and controls all things. He is the ruler of the entire universe; He reigns above all creatures, substances, particles, and things. Our God is all that we could ever imagine and so much more. We are reminded of His closeness today. The writer of Psalm 138 tells us "though the Lord is on high, he looks upon the lowly" (vs. 6). Our God is not too big or too busy to watch over us. Just as a parent keeps their eyes on their children, our God looks after us. "The Lord watches over you...the Lord will watch over your coming and going both now and forevermore" (Psalm 121:5, 8).

Because God watches over you, He sees the things that you go through. He sees when you're in need. He sees your hurt, pain, and suffering. He sees and He responds. The psalm writer said "though I walk in the midst of trouble, you preserve my life; you stretch out your hand against the anger of my foes with you right hand you save me" (vs. 7). God sees your need and sends help. He does not leave you in the midst of trouble, hurt, or enemy attack, but compassionately reaches down from His throne to save you. God comes for His children!

Psalm 34:17-20 says:

"The righteous cry out, and the Lord hears them;
  he delivers them from all their troubles.
The Lord is close to the brokenhearted
  and saves those who are crushed in spirit.
The righteous person may have many troubles,
  but the Lord delivers him from them all;
he protects all his bones,
  not one of them will be broken."

No matter what circumstance you face today, remember that your God is still on throne. Although it may look rough or tough, take heart. You are not alone. The enemy may be after you; you may feel pressed on every side, but "be strong and courageous. Do not be afraid or terrified because of them, for the

Lord your God goes with you; he will never leave you nor forsake you" (Deuteronomy 31:6).

Psalm 139

Today, we are reminded of just how intimately we are known by God. God knows us better than any other person on this earth, including us. Yes, God knows us better than we know ourselves. We know our thoughts, our emotions, and even our bodies, but we have blind spots. We often struggle to identify the source of certain thoughts. Has something every run across your mind and you were left saying, "Where did that come from?" We often wrestle to label the emotions that we experience. Maybe you've said, "I can't explain what I am feeling, but something just isn't right." Sometimes, we are even unable to qualify the sensations of our bodies. Have you set at the doctor attempting to complete a form and couldn't decide whether to check the "numb, tingling, stabbing, piercing or burning box" as the type of pain you were experiencing? Although we know ourselves, our knowledge is imperfect. But God knows us perfectly.

God knows every move we make. The psalm writer says, "You know when I sit and when I rise" "you discern my going out and my lying down; you are familiar with all my ways" (vs. 2, 3). We often walk around feeling like no one sees us. No one sees our hearts. No one sees our efforts. No one sees us for who we really are. But, God sees me and He sees you. What good news! Our God is omniscient. He knows everything. He has infinite awareness, knowledge, and understanding and He uses this awareness to watch over you. Psalm 32:8 says that God keeps His eye on you. God sees us when we're hurt, sad, struggling, and in pain. He also sees us when we are happy, excited, and having a good day. God sees us and responds; He follows us. Nothing can separate us from God. Verses 8-10 tell us that God will meet us wherever we go; "If I go up to the heavens, you are there; if I make my bed in the depths, you are there. If I rise on the wings of the dawn, if I settle on the far side of the sea, even there your hand will guide me, your right hand will hold me fast." Even when you feel that no one sees you or that you have even stepped outside of the boundaries of God's reach, remember that neither is possible. There is nowhere you can go that our omniscient God does not see or will not come after you.

God knows our every thought, even before they take shape. "You perceive my thoughts from afar" "before a word is on my tongue you know it completely, O Lord" (vs. 2, 4). Before we have awareness of our thoughts and before our thoughts transform into words, God knows them. God's omniscience extends to our innermost being. Even our poker face cannot hide our thoughts from God. God actively discerns us. We cannot hide from God or the reach of His Spirit. David, the writer of this psalm, was amazed by this fact. He asked, "Where can I go from your Spirit? Where can I flee from your presence?" (vs. 7) Nowhere. People like to say, "You are what you think"; God knows us most intimately because He knows what we think even before we do. God knows you; the real you. There is nowhere that you can hide from God. God has searched you and He knows you (vs. 1).

God knows us best because He made us. "For you created my inmost being; you knit me together in my mother's womb" (vs. 13). God chose every detail about you; you were custom made. There is no one on earth that is quite like you. God gave you your own DNA, personality, gifts, talents, calling, and anointing. It was all knit-together by God. God knew us, before we did. And as we continue to learn ourselves, discover our capabilities, and come into our own, only God holds the answer to the question "who am I?" As you seek to know you, seek God. He already knows you.

It is awesome to serve a God who knows us so intimately; who makes it His business to keep up with our thoughts, our feelings, and our actions.

Psalm 140

We meet David today in the midst of a prayer for deliverance from evil. He is surrounded by violence, slander, and wicked schemes. Thousands of years later, this sounds all too familiar, doesn't it? We still experience wars, rumors of wars, sabotage, senseless killings, and financial scams—all flowing from the hearts of evil men and women. Mothers are killing their children, police are striking down innocent people, coaches are abusing their players, and mentors are taking advantage of mentees. Although the date on the calendar has changed, the truth has not—evil walks among us in human flesh. Some people are simply evil--they act maliciously. David was not seeking deliverance from accidental wrongdoers. No these men plotted from their hearts and used their tongues, hands, and feet to bring others down.

The people after David must have been dreadful because David compared them to serpents and vipers (vs. 3). In the natural realm, both serpents and vipers are poisonous snakes. They crawl around on their bellies poisoning anything or anyone that they can sink their teeth in, acting even without provocation. If bitten by these creatures, you will surely die (without intervention of a healer). This explains why David cried out "rescue me, O Lord, from evil men; protect me from men of violence" (vs. 1). David knew that without the Lord's help these men would take his life. Biblically, the serpent is synonymous with Satan who is vengeful and vindictive. He tempted Adam and Eve in Genesis 3, attempted to tempt Jesus in Matthew 4, and will come after you before you know it. He means you no good, but only comes around to steal, kill, and destroy (John 10:10). Satan sets trap for us, enticing us to fall into his schemes, leading us further and further away from the path and plan that God has for us. The men after David did the same; "proud men have hidden a snare for me; they have spread out the cords of their net and have set straps for me along my path" (vs. 5). We must be careful to avoid Satan and his schemes and evil men and women who are like him.

Even though you may find yourself surrounded by evil men and women and the traps of Satan, there is good news. "God is faithful; he will not let you be tempted beyond what you can bear. But when you are tempted, he will also provide a way out so that you can endure it" (1 Corinthians 10:13). The traps and snares will be set, the attempts to take your life and destroy everything connected to it will be made, slanderous tongues will wag, but they will not take you out. God will provide a way out so that you can endure the temptation of the enemy. David knew this and cried out to God for help. He knew that God would lead him through the valley, so he had nothing to fear and stood on that confidence during this trial (Psalm 23).

You may encounter evil men and women today. The enemy will try to steal, kill, or destroy you, your family, your finances, your home or something else that you hold dear. But know that as long as the Lord is on the throne that you are covered. God will help you to endure and secure justice on your behalf (vs. 13).

Psalm 141

Today, the psalm writer lifts up a prayer to God that we rarely pray. David asked the Lord to keep him from desiring, doing, and speaking evil. David did not ask for material things, blessings, or His favor today, he asked God to help him to avoid compromise. "Set a guard over my mouth, O Lord; keep watch over the door of my lips. Let not my heart be drawn to what is evil, to take part in wicked deeds" (vs. 3-4). David wanted to remain righteous and therefore did not want to be drawn to evil things and people.

David's concern about being tempted by evil was so strong that he asked God to send righteous men and women to discipline him when necessary. "Let a righteous man strike me—it is a kindness; let him rebuke me—it is oil on my head. My head will not refuse it" (vs. 5). How many of us ask to be disciplined? How often does a child request a spanking or to sit in time-out? Almost never, right? The psalm writer knew that discipline is ultimately for our good and flows from a heart of love. David knew the truth of Hebrews 12:6-11; "'the Lord disciplines the one he loves, and he chastens everyone he accepts as his son.' Endure hardship as discipline; God is treating you as his children. For what children are not disciplined by their father? If you are not disciplined—and everyone undergoes discipline—then you are not legitimate, not true sons and daughters at all. Moreover, we have all had human fathers who disciplined us and we respected them for it. How much more should we submit to the Father of spirits and live! They disciplined us for a little while as they thought best; but God disciplines us for our good, in order that we may share in His holiness. No discipline seems pleasant at the time, but painful. Later on, however, it produces a harvest of righteousness and peace for those who have been trained by it."

The prayer of this psalm came from the lips of a spiritually mature man. David desired to please God and knew that obedience to God's commandments was vitally important to do so (John 14:15). God and His discipline help us to live righteously. Remember to ask God to keep you away from those things that hinder your walk and lead you towards things that will strengthen it.

Psalm 142

Today, David is still struggling with enemies who are after him. He is in dire need of a move of God. He cries out "listen to my cry, for I am in desperate need; rescue me from those who pursue me, for they are too strong for me" (vs. 6-7). I feel bad for David. It seems that his enemies' pursuit is unending and merciless. Day in and day out, they taunt him, mock him, stalk him, attack his reputation and attempt to kill him. Who can stand under this sort of persecution? David is tired of his reality; he prays "set me free from my prison, that I may praise your name" (vs. 7). He simply wants out.

I cannot begin to imagine living this sort of life. Can you? Most of us struggle if too many people are gossiping about us or if one person at work is plotting our ruin or if two people at church are committed to making us look bad. Most of us have never and will never experience David's reality--daily persecution on every side and death threats. Unfortunately, there was more; David was going through this alone. "Look to my right and see; no one is concerned for me. I have no refuge; no one cares for my life" (vs. 4). He told us in Psalm 27:10 that both his mother and father had forsaken him. In Psalm 55:12-14 he tells us about his friends; "if an enemy were insulting me, I could endure it; if a foe were rising against me, I could hide. But it is you, a man like myself, my companion, my close friend, with whom I once enjoyed sweet fellowship at the house of God, as we walked about among the worshipers." His friends had become his enemies and his parents had abandoned him, David walked alone and no one seemed to care.

Although we may not have experienced David's situation specifically, we have felt abandoned, forsaken, and alone. We know what it is like to feel as if no one cares about our pains, hurts, struggles, or problems. Have you called every person that you have on speed-dial only to find that they were unavailable or unconcerned about your needs? This is the place that we meet David in Psalm 142. I imagine him weeping and curled up on the ground in a fetal position as he prayed before the Lord. You've been there, right?

David lamented in verse 4 that he had no refuge and then declared in verse 5, "you are my refuge, my portion in the land of the living." After you cried your tears, shared your hurt, devastation, and disappointment with God, and came out of the little ball on the floor, what did you do next? Did you ask God to be what you needed? Not simply to supply your needs, but to be what you were lacking, missing, or thirsting for? David did. Psalm 73:26 says, God IS the strength of your heart and Psalm 16:5 says, God IS your portion and cup (emphasis mine). God is prepared to be everything you need. The next time you find yourself overcome by feelings of abandonment or forsakenness remember that God is there. You are never alone, because God IS always there.

Yes, David is still dealing with his enemies. I know you are wondering what else we can possibly learn from yet another psalm about this man running from his enemies. The thing that God asked me to highlight today actually has little to do with David or his enemies. ☺ So take a deep breath.

Re-read the psalm. Now stop at verse 11. David said, "For your name's sake, O Lord, preserve my life." David's focus is on God. In fact, everything is all about God; about His reputation, about Him receiving glory and about God being honored through the David's life. Although David was going through a great trial, ultimately it was not about David, but about God.

David was a servant of the Lord. As a result, his life was like a traffic sign pointing back to God. During Old Testament times, it was believed that a person's god was in control of everything concerning them. That god provided, healed, protected, delivered, saved, and otherwise directed one's life. If David was victorious, the victory would be attributed to God. If he was defeated, that too would be credited to Him. Likewise, the god of a defeated person was deemed weak and powerless, while the victor's god was strong and mighty. So, what David was going through was more about God than it was about David. David's life may have been at stake, but God's name was on the line.

The same is true of our lives. Our lives are like traffic signs pointing beyond us to God. As children, our parents warned us not to bring embarrassment to them through our actions. Why? They knew that if we misbehaved it would say something about them as parents. Their names were at stake when we went to school, church, play-dates, and other places. John 1:12 says that by believing in Jesus we became children of God. Romans 8:14-17 says, if we are children then we are heirs. Ephesians 1:13 says, God marked us. We represent God in the world. When we act and speak, God's name is at stake. Your life is not really about you, but all about God. Everything is about God.

As you go through this day, pray as David did "teach me to do your will" (vs. 10). David understood that his life was not his own, but a sign pointing back to God. By doing God's will, God would be glorified through him. Ask God to help you to speak and act in such a way today that men and women will see God's love, compassion, goodness, and mercy.

Psalm 144

Although the attacks of David's enemies had not subsided, he continued to pray to the Lord for wisdom and help. In response, God encouraged David. As we meet him in the prayer of Psalm 144, it seems that God gave David fresh revelation about his situation. David cried out, "Praise be to the Lord my Rock, who trains my hands for war, my fingers for battle" (vs. 1). As David lamented about his enemies and their attacks, God replied "I have prepared you for this."

While David experienced spiritual and verbal assaults, he was always in imminent danger of bodily harm and death. David dodged spears, knives, swords, and everything in between. He hid in caves and deserts as he fled his home running for his life. His enemies weren't simply trying to hurt his reputation; they were trying to take him out! As David cried out to the Lord in fear, God responded, "you can handle this battle; you were trained for such a time as this." David was a mighty warrior. He not only killed Goliath in 1 Samuel 17, but subsequently led Israel in battle after battle. He was a skillful warrior and mighty in battle. It was prophesied of David, " 'Saul has slain his thousands, and David his tens of thousands'" (1 Samuel 18:7). Every battle had prepared David for the ultimate war—the war to save his life.

The same is true for you. God has not only prepared you for the battle you are currently in, but will prepare you for the war that will surely come. God knows the way you will take and has prepared you to succeed (Job 23:10). The attack on David's life may have come as a surprise to him, but it did not catch God off guard. God knows when a storm is on the horizon in your life and has already sent an umbrella to cover you. He knows when the enemy will attack and has already placed restrictions on what he can and cannot do to you. Our Father is aware of the challenges on your job, in your relationships, and with your health. He has trained your hands for war and fingers for battle. You will overcome.

Psalm 145

One of the good things about reading the Bible is that the writers give us great insight into the character of God. Often this is done when the writer brags about who God has been to them. Today, we learn more about God through David's praise:

- **God is the King** (vs. 1)
- **God performs mighty acts** (vs. 4)
- **He is majestic** (vs. 5)
- **His works are powerful and awesome** (vs. 6)
- **The Lord is gracious and compassionate** (vs. 8)
- **God is good to all** (vs. 9)
- **His kingdom is glorious** (vs. 11)
- **His kingdom is everlasting** (vs. 13)
- **His dominion is enduring** (vs. 13)
- **The Lord is faithful and loving** (vs. 13)
- **He upholds the bowed down** (vs. 14)
- **He is a provider** (vs. 15)
- **God is righteous** (vs. 17)
- **He is near to those who call upon Him** (vs. 18)
- **He fulfills the desires of those who fear Him** (vs. 19)
- **He hears our cries and saves us** (vs. 19)
- **He watches over those who love Him** (vs. 20)

David shares eighteen characteristics of the Lord in this psalm. Knowing God comes through time and experience with Him, just as it does in human relationships. The more time that we spend with God, the more we will learn about Him; the more that He will reveal Himself to us. The longer that we walk closely with God, the more opportunities to know Him will present themselves.

Of all the characteristics that David presented in this psalm, which two are most unfamiliar to you? List them below:

1.

2.

Which of these qualities have you not seen in your relationship with God? List two below:

1.

2.

After picking the characteristics that you are most unfamiliar with and haven't seen in your relationship, ask God to demonstrate them to you. Persist in asking until He reveals Himself in these ways. Paul said, in Philippians 3:10-11, "I want to know Christ—yes, to know the power of his resurrection and participation in his sufferings, becoming like him in his death, and so, somehow, attaining to the resurrection from the dead." What is it that you want to personally know about God? Nothing tops a personal experience with and of God.

Psalm 146

Today, the psalmist calls us to place our trust in God instead of human beings. He says, "Do not put your trust in princes, in human beings, who cannot save. When their spirit departs, they return to the ground; on that very day their plans come to nothing. Blessed are those whose help is the God of Jacob, whose hope is in the Lord their God" (vs. 5-7). Even when our intentions are good, human ability is limited, but God possesses unlimited power.

We shift personal responsibility for our lives and circumstances to the other people when we place too much trust in humans. Only you and God are ultimately responsible for you. We should be able to trust those with whom we are in relationship with not to hurt us, abuse us, or harm us, but we should only place a healthy dose of confidence in another human. Placing our faith and trust in someone other than God is a recipe for personal failure. Humans will disappoint you, take advantage of you, ignore your needs, forget your preferences, and otherwise disregard you. But God is always faithful, reliable, trustworthy, gracious, merciful, and compassionate.

Flip back to the characteristics of God that we studied yesterday in Psalm 145. What person do you know who is all of those things at all times? You may be able to name people who are some of those things most of the time. But only God possesses the ability to display all of those characteristics at all times. Humans are limited, while God is unlimited. "Trust in the Lord with all your heart and lean not on your own understanding; in all your ways submit to him, and he will make your paths straight" (Proverbs 3:5-6). Notice that the writer did not say for us to trust in our mother, father, sister, brother, friend, pastor, or co-worker. He said to trust in the Lord; God will always have your back.

Psalm 147

Today, we learn more about the power of God's Word. When God speaks, things happen. Things change. People respond. The earth reacts. What other person's word holds that type of weight? When I speak, a few may listen, a couple may react, and even a handful may obey. There is always a reaction to the Word of the Lord. The writer of Psalm 147:15-17 says "He sends his command to the earth; his word runs swiftly. He spreads the snow like wool and scatters the frost like ashes. He hurls down his hail like pebbles. Who can withstand his icy blast? He sends his word and melts them; he stirs up his breezes, and the waters flow."

You may be the boss on your job. You may be the pastor of a great congregation. You may be the leader of a ministry. You may be the head of a household. You may be the oldest sibling. People may respond to your commands, demands, requests, and your word, but when was the last time that something you said made ice melt, caused a breeze to blow, or made water flow? Really? Our God is so powerful that even the words from His mouth bring transformation and change.

The same authority that God uses to command the earth, spread snow, scatter frost, and hurl hail, will also be used to protect you, comfort you, care for you, deliver you, provide for you, and meet every other need you have. "He will command his angels concerning you to guard you in all your ways" (Psalm 91:11). "The Lord will send a blessing on your barns and on everything you put your hand to" (Deuteronomy 28:8). He will send out his Word to heal and rescue you (Psalm 107:20). God will speak on your behalf and the atmosphere will change, situations will align, people will submit, demons will tremble and the devil will flee all because God spoke that thing concerning you. God's Word will never fail you. "For as the rain and the snow come down from heaven, And do not return there without watering the earth And making it bear and sprout, And furnishing seed to the sower and bread to the eater; So will My word be which goes forth from My mouth; It will not return to Me empty, Without accomplishing what I desire, And without succeeding in the matter for which I sent it" (Isaiah 55:10-11).

Thank God for His Word today! Thank God for His faithfulness to speak words to prosper you and to give you hope and a future (Jeremiah 29:11)! God is always interceding on your behalf; trust that when He speaks your life will never be the same.

Psalm 148

Today, the psalmist calls for all created things to praise the Lord. He declares that from the heavens to the earth, from the water to the skies, from nation to nation, God is worthy of praise! It was God who created all things and ensured their ability to withstand the tests and trials of time; "for at his command they were created, and he established them for ever and ever—he issued a decree that will never pass away" (vs. 5-6). We were built to last. Oh what good news that is for us! Humans were not created to last for a single generation, but from generation to generation to generation. The stars were not created to evaporate after only a century. The ocean was not designed to dry up after three decades. Everything God created was set in place to be here until the end of time.

What does that mean for you? It means that God did not allow you to be tempted in order for you to give in, but He planned for you to endure. "No temptation has overtaken you except what is common to mankind. And God is faithful; he will not let you be tempted beyond what you can bear. But when you are tempted, he will also provide a way out so that you can endure it" (1 Corinthians 10:13). God did not allow a battle to be waged against you for you to be defeated, but He planned for you to be victorious. "You will not have to fight this battle. Take up your positions; stand firm and see the deliverance the Lord will give you, Judah and Jerusalem. Do not be afraid; do not be discouraged. Go out to face them tomorrow, and the Lord will be with you" (2 Chronicles 20:17). God did not allow that sickness to touch your body to destroy you, because He desires for you to prosper. "Dear friend, I pray that you may enjoy good health and that all may go well with you, even as your soul is getting along well" (3 John 1:2). You were built to withstand anything that life, flesh, or the enemy could throw your way. You were also built to endure everything that God allows you to encounter on the path in which He leads you.

No matter what you are going through, know that you will make it to the other side. God built you to last, to endure, to withstand. Praise God in the midst of it all. Even if you feel alone, know that you are not. God has given you endless praise partners in His creation. Everything around you was build to last and has been called forth to praise the Lord. Join the sun and moon, sea creatures and ocean depths, trees and cedars, and small creatures and flying birds in giving God praise today.

Psalm 149

The psalmist continues his instruction on praise today. He begins with his customary call to "Praise the Lord" in verse 1 and then continues on to offer us various methods to glorify God. First, we are called to offer God a new song, that is to give God something fresh, novel, and different. Our 'ol faithful hymns and praise choruses definitely have their place in worship and are received by God, but sometimes we need to say something different, do something different, express something different. Just as I would get tired of hearing the same song over and over and over again, I would imagine that my singing the same tune could get a little old for God too. God continues to reveal Himself to us in new and different ways. I challenge you to find different ways to express your praise back to Him. The next time you prepare to offer God praise, try to find new songs, write your own poems, psalms or songs, or even offer God a different dance.

The psalmist moves on to tell us that praise is both a corporate and private matter. We often only offer God praise while we are at church or gathered with other believers, but the psalmist calls us to offer God "praise in the assembly" in verse 1 and on our beds in verse 5. Just as the Bible teaches us to pray in corporate and private settings, we are called to praise in both places as well. Matthew 6:6 says "But when you pray, go into your room, close the door and pray to your Father, who is unseen. Then your Father, who sees what is done in secret, will reward you." Matthew is not telling us that public prayer is inappropriate, but addresses the motives of our prayers. He was calling people to avoid praying to be seen. Both corporate and private prayers are vital to our spiritual growth and development. James calls us to corporate prayer in James 5:14-16 "Is anyone among you sick? Let them call the elders of the church to pray over them and anoint them with oil in the name of the Lord. And the prayer offered in faith will make the sick person well; the Lord will raise them up. If they have sinned, they will be forgiven. Therefore confess your sins to each other and pray for each other so that you may be healed. The prayer of a righteous person is powerful and effective." Just as we need private and public prayer, the writer of Psalm 149 teaches us that there is a time for both private and corporate praise as well.

Take time to assess your "praise life" today. Which area needs to be strengthened? Do you need to strive to find new ways to offer God praise? Maybe a new song, poem, or dance is in order. Do you need to work on joining your congregation in praise on Sunday mornings? Maybe it has been a spectator sport for you in the past, but you need to push yourself to become engaged by standing, bowing, lifting your hands, clapping, dancing, singing, or rocking. Do you need to make praise apart of your private time with God? Maybe you need to start journaling your words of praise, listening to music, singing, playing instruments, or dancing at home. Commit to respond to the challenge of Psalm 149 today in whatever way that God leads you.

Psalm 150

As the psalmist lifts up his final Psalm of Praise, he provides us with comprehensive instruction on the subject matter. While we learned a great deal about praising God from previous psalms, this one brings all of those lessons together into one place. We learned about demonstrative praise in Psalm 98. He taught us some of the reasons that God is worthy of praise in Psalm 99. Psalm 100 taught us about our posture as we enter the temple. We learned in Psalm 149 about the places that we are to praise God. This psalm covers each of these areas; this is the "who," "what," "when," "where," and "how" of praise.

The "who" is simple; God is to be praised. We are called to "Praise the Lord" (vs. 1). Jesus reminds us while being tempted by Satan that only God deserves our praise, worship, and service. "Jesus answered, It is written: 'Worship the Lord your God and serve him only'" (Luke 4:8).

With "what" are we called to praise God? We are to praise God with whatever we have access to and within us. The psalm writer calls us to use trumpets, harps, lyres, tambourines, strings, flutes, and symbols in Psalm 150. All instruments, both external and internal, can be used to give God praise. Unfortunately, some believe that certain instruments are off-limits, but the Bible shows no condemnation of any instrument or particular tool for praising God. We can use candles, artwork, pictures, bodies, incense, and a plethora of other things to glorify, magnify and lift up the name of God. While the Bible does not restrict "what" we use to praise God, it calls us to praise and worship God at all times, in all things and most importantly in spirit and in truth (1 Thessalonians 5:15, John 4:24). Don't get caught up in the "what"; use pots, pans, and spoons if you must, but praise Him!

The psalmist does not specifically address the "when" of praise in this psalm, but if you read Psalm 149 and 150 together you will have the answer to when praise is appropriate. We are to praise God in the morning and evening. We are to praise Him in good times and bad. The writer of Psalm 34:1 declares "I will bless the Lord at all times: his praise shall continually be in my mouth" (King James Version). We should join the psalm writer in ceaseless praise of an awesome God, who is worthy of our praise.

"Where" should we offer God praise? Everywhere. Praise should extend from the heavens above to the earth below. The psalm writer called us to "Praise God in his sanctuary; praise him in his mighty heavens" (vs. 1). Every place that God created is a good place for His praises to be sang, spoken, danced, played, and otherwise lifted. Psalm 148 called for praise in the skies and waters (vs. 3-4), in the mountains and hills (vs. 9), in the oceans (vs. 7) and on earth throughout all nations (vs. 11). God's praise can be lifted and should be lifted up everywhere!

Finally, "how." How are we to praise God? The sky is the limit. We can praise God through song, dance, spoken word, drama, painting, and any other form that brings Him glory. We are called to praise the Lord from the inside out; from our souls. "Praise the Lord, my soul; all my inmost being, praise his holy name" (Psalm 103:1). We have been charged to lift up holy hands to God (1 Timothy 2:8). Psalm 95:6 calls us to kneel before God. God has given us freedom to express our adoration of Him. We are free to worship and praise in Jesus name. "Now the Lord is the Spirit, and where the Spirit of the Lord is, there is freedom" (2 Corinthians 3:17). Walk in your liberty and freedom today and everyday, henceforth, now and forevermore!

Conclusion

I pray that this devotional journey has helped you to draw nearer to God. Hopefully you have received revelation from God that has blessed your life, strengthen your walk, and encouraged your soul. The psalm writers were people dealing with the same types of issues, emotions, and circumstances that each of us experience at various points throughout our walk with God. It is often helpful to hear someone express exactly what we are feeling; the Book of Psalms provides us with a knowing voice. The Psalms also provide us with insight into the heart, mind, will, and character of God while providing us with instruction that guides our walk with the Lord. I encourage you to keep these 150 chapters at the top of your mind, heart, and soul as you continue your journey with the Lord.

God Bless You.
Love, Leah